The Challenge of Hunger

THE CHALLENGE OF HUNGER

A Program for More Effective Foreign Aid

I. W. MOOMAW

FREDERICK A. PRAEGER, *Publishers*
New York · Washington · London

FREDERICK A. PRAEGER, PUBLISHERS
111 Fourth Avenue, New York, N.Y. 10003, U.S.A.
77–79 Charlotte Street, London, W.1, England

Published in the United States of America in 1966
by Frederick A. Praeger, Inc., Publishers

Library of Congress Catalog Card Number: 66-13670

Printed in the United States of America

"We must work with the precision of the jeweler,
the vision of the prophet, and the strength of the giant."

—SARVEPALLI RADHAKRISHNAN
President of India

PREFACE

MOST AMERICANS would agree that foreign aid in some form will be with us for many years. The spreading anguish of world hunger, the demand of more than a billion people for a better life, and the pressures for violent revolution make this imperative. The only questions are: What kind of aid? How much? How shall it be administered?

The widespread dissatisfaction with our present foreign-aid program, both at home and overseas, reflects deep and unresolved defects. The Critical Issues Council, in its report of July, 1964, said that "without fundamental changes, the program will still be floundering five years hence, if indeed, the American people have not scrapped it in disgust."

What are the fundamental changes for which friends of the foreign-aid idea are calling? There are no simple answers, but we do have access to a vast fund of information and experience. More than 10,000 Americans have been abroad on assignments since the program began as Point Four. Among them have been some of our most able scientists and administrators. An even larger number of citizens of host countries have participated in the program. In preparing this book, I have drawn heavily upon the views of these experienced men and women.

It is a pleasure to acknowledge the help I have received from various sources. Peasant farmers in many countries spoke freely about their problems, hopes, and disappointments. Officers of U.S. AID in Washington and abroad were generous in sharing information.

A panel of twenty well-informed men and women read the manuscript and made comments and criticisms. Kenneth L. Maxwell, Director for International Affairs, National Council of Churches; Raymond W. Miller, Guest Lecturer at the Graduate School of Business Administration, Harvard University; J. Benton Rhoades, Executive Secretary of Agricultural Missions, Inc.; and William H. Stacy (retired), Rural Sociologist at Iowa State University, assisted regularly as consultants during the study.

Mrs. Ward Shoemaker gave generously of her time for research and help in preparing the manuscript. I am especially indebted to Edward R. Sammis for his inspiration and professional assistance as consulting editor. I am grateful to my wife for her help in securing field materials and for her careful reading of the manuscript.

Because of the overriding importance of better farming and stronger village institutions as the basis for progress, I have devoted the largest amount of space to agriculture and rural development. At some points I have written critically, but I hope that my appreciation of AID's accomplishments and my desire to see a more effective program come through clearly.

There will inevitably be differences of opinion on such a complex and controversial issue, but if the book in some measure leads to a more effective foreign-aid program my purpose will have been fulfilled.

I. W. Moomaw

Lancaster, Pennsylvania
January, 1966

CONTENTS

The Challenge of Hunger

1

FOREIGN AID AT THE CROSSROADS

ONLY A dozen years ago, our foreign aid program, then known as Point Four, was acclaimed by most Americans as "the finest foreign policy gesture in our history." Since then, it has become one of our most controversial issues.

On December 24, 1963, in a dramatic predawn session, the House of Representatives gave our foreign aid budget the deepest cut in its stormy history.

Even though President Kennedy, of his own volition, had reduced the $5 billion he had originally requested to $4.5 billion, the Eighty-eighth Congress held the 1964 budget under heated discussion for more than five weeks. In the revised budget, $2 billion had been requested for military aid; the remaining $2.5 billion was for economic assistance to underdeveloped countries.

When the congressmen walked down the Capitol steps that morning, their business was done. The military appropriation was allowed to stand. But economic assistance had been cut to $1 billion. This amount was 60 per cent below the sum President Kennedy had designated as "the bare minimum essential to meet our obligations to the developing nations."

This move came as the climax to long months of debate during which foreign aid had come under increasingly bitter attack.

In the summer of 1963, a public-opinion poll showed that only 58 per cent of those Americans questioned favored foreign aid of any kind. On the floor of Congress, voices were raised which reflected the concern of constituents back home. Senator Wayne Morse, a friend of the foreign aid idea, declared with his usual forthrightness: "The American taxpayers are being rooked by our world-wide giveaway program!" In another speech from the Senate floor, he said: "Finally, I would revise the entire basis for foreign aid. I would terminate all current aid except for irrevocable commitments, on June 30, 1965."

The news media joined the general protest. Typical of the acid comments is this excerpt from an editorial in the Maine *Bangor Daily News* of December 19, 1963: "Much of it [foreign aid] has served to bolster up the political, if not the personal, fortunes of leaders in aided countries, while giving little, if any help to the needy masses."

What had happened?

Originally the churches and civic groups had pledged their vigorous moral support. The great farm organizations were solidly behind it. Developing nations welcomed it with hope and gratitude.

Now, however, both public opinion and the mood of the Congress seemed to have swung heavily to the opposition. Certain congressmen and editorial writers flatly stated that they would like to see foreign aid brought to an end altogether. Many there were who wanted to see it cut back. Even President Johnson, in his message to Congress defending his 1964 budget for foreign aid, suggested that the staff be reduced by 1,200 before the close of 1965.

All of us who had been working closely to foreign aid

had become worried over the growing disenchantment with the program. But the December 24 budget cut came as a sharp warning that the very life of the program was now in danger.

Foreign aid was clearly at the crossroads. Either it would have to regain public confidence, or it would flounder toward a disastrous end. To me this was a stunning blow, for I had a deep personal interest in foreign aid from the day Point Four was announced.

I was born and grew up on an Ohio farm. In 1924, soon after graduation from Ohio State, I found myself in India, at work on a program of agricultural and rural development supported by the Church of the Brethren. I continued in this work for the next twenty years. During that period, I saw Indian villagers form one of the first successful cooperatives with a capital of $50; valiant missionaries struggled to free peasants from the age-old grip of the usurer.

Our resources in those days in both personnel and funds were meager. We were continually haunted by unmet, heartbreaking human needs. During that period, one became all too familiar with the bare struggle to exist on the part of millions.

In 1946, my work took on a broader aspect when I was called to the national office of Agricultural Missions, Inc., in New York.* From that time on, periodic field trips took me to nearly all of the major countries with which we now have foreign aid programs.

With each journey, I became more aware of the enormous job to be done, and the short time in which to do it. Even then it took no special imagination to foresee the mounting problem of world hunger in all its urgent proportions.

I, along with all other agricultural missionaries, rejoiced when Point Four was announced. Here at last the attack on want could be launched in a manner and on a scale which the job merited!

* Agricultural Missions, Inc. is a service organization for churches and private agencies devoted to agricultural improvement in depressed areas around the world.

In addition to my interest in the program, I had many friends in the U.S. Department of Agriculture and in agricultural colleges who were among the first to join Point Four and go abroad. Therefore, it was only natural that on routine visits I met these people and learned of their difficulties and successes. In 1953, by invitation from the office of U.S. AID in Washington, I gave special attention to visiting projects in the Middle East and Asia, and presented a written report when I returned home. This I did in the course of my regular duties.

As the years went by, many of us became deeply disturbed by disappointments abroad as well as dissatisfaction at home over the achievements in foreign aid. We saw that this undertaking, once so popular, was failing to measure up to the early expectations as a bold new program.

So, in the summer of 1963, I again gave special attention to meeting both U.S. foreign aid specialists and leaders in other countries in an effort to learn what might be done toward bringing the program more nearly in line with its original aims.

Many of the attainments should be a source of pride to any American. Among them were low-cost housing projects, rural youth clubs, courses for leader training, and school lunches for children.

But perhaps the most significant impression one received was the mood of confidence among villagers, farmers, and leaders who told of the checking of malaria, better crop yields, and the building of new irrigation systems. Above all, many expressed their conviction that a better future was within reach, if not for themselves, at least for their children.

Evidence of the need for foreign aid was everywhere. I was walking along the main street in Lahore, Pakistan, for example, at about the time the program was being bitterly attacked in Congress.

I was fascinated by the variety of vehicles inching their way among the pedestrians. A few automobiles maneuvered incongruously around slow-moving bullock teams. Bicycles wove in and out. Sweating men were pushing carts loaded with bags of grain and cement. Along the sidewalks, vendors hawked glass bangles, handmade toys, ready-cooked rice, and sweetmeats from their big, flat baskets.

A small cart drawn by two reddish-brown ponies passed by. The driver finished eating an orange, and tossed the last bit, with the peeling still on it, into the street.

As though from nowhere, five barefoot boys appeared, leaped for it, and struggled over it until it was gone. One little fellow wore only a tattered, waist-length shirt. Because he was small, he couldn't get close enough to the orange peel to touch it. With a gesture of resignation, he turned and trudged back to the curb.

It was midmorning. I thought that these lads should have been in school. But they had a more immediate need. Here, on my first day in Pakistan, although I knew the food shortage was not as acute as in many places, I was reminded of the growing threat of hunger to the peace and stability of the world. The scene haunted me. Hunger speaks with an eloquent tongue when you meet it face-to-face.

A few days later, I walked with an American doctor as he made his rounds through a great church-supported hospital in Multan. I asked him if there were any diseases peculiar to the country and its climate. "One: hunger," he said. "Most of the people I am treating would not be here at all if they had enough to eat."

On the verandah the shriveled and motionless form of a boy lay on a cot. His big, deep-sunken eyes stared at me as though from the face of an old man. His white teeth looked like those in a skull. His bloated stomach billowed out below his bony rib case. I had often seen *kwashiorkor,* the dreaded hunger disease of children, but I had never seen anything like this.

"He's nine years old and weighs twenty-six pounds," the doctor explained.

"Can he ever get well?"

"Oh, yes, he does fine so long as he's here. We give him vitamin injections and feed him up on malt extract with milk and fruit juices. But what's the use if he can't get food after he leaves? Pakistan has more than two million children on the brink of starvation."

"Who is he?" I asked.

"His name is Ahmed," the doctor replied. "A pastor brought him in. He lives with his parents on the edge of town, in a shack made of tin and fodder stalks. His father has been out of work for months. Ahmed was starving." We moved on; piercing eyes followed us.

That afternoon, with the specters of Ahmed and the boys struggling for the orange peeling still very much in mind, I went to keep an appointment with Pakistan's Deputy Minister for Land Settlement.

I was aware that some people at home were objecting to foreign aid because they felt that certain countries were leaning on us too heavily, and that by helping them, we were doing only what they themselves could and ought to be doing.

Papers from home evinced considerable concern over the growing rapport between Pakistan and Red China, and the mounting dissension with India over Kashmir. But nowhere did I find any word about the more intensive struggle going on in Pakistan, the effort to bring land into production fast enough to feed the expanding population. It was that struggle which held my interest, for I knew that, compassion aside, freedom from hunger and political freedom were inseparable.

The deputy, a serious man, looked at me from deep-set eyes across a table stacked with reports. Two assistants standing nearby were rustling papers in an effort to catch his attention. Outside, a dozen or so men were standing about under a tree. The deputy told me he had just returned from a tour of inspection of those arid lands which make up much of the area of West Pakistan.

"My idea of heaven," he said with a sigh, "would be some day to be able to convert those gray, sandy wastes into little green farms, each with its garden patch, its rice field, its well, its orchard, and its tidy home. We're gaining, we still have hope, but we know it's going to take time and will cost a lot of money. It *must* be done, you know."

A movement in the crowd under the trees attracted his eye. He glanced out the window.

"They wait—they always wait," he said. "I marvel that they do not despair. They weigh heavily on a man's conscience. Can you imagine what it means to have over a million landless farmers, all looking to *you* to see that they get some bit of soil they can till and call their own?"

Here was a situation I was finding not unusual in developing countries where a number of men in responsible posts are under pressure to solve centuries-old social and economic problems overnight. And as they strain to do their utmost, they are ever conscious of the threat of revolution facing them if they fail.

They, far more than ourselves, I thought, are aware of the growing insistence of the hungry, the untaught, the oppressed, that something must be done, and done soon, to better the lot of these awakening millions.

It occurred to me that a visible and dramatic danger inspires men to action. But hunger, the cruelest of all foes because it strikes against the defenseless—against children and women—is a slow and quiet enemy. The starving do not march. They suffer in silence until the moment comes when they explode in the violence of desperation.

One could see that there was no quick or easy palliative to the problems posed to foreign aid. To bring barren land into production, for example, could not, as the deputy had pointed out, be accomplished overnight. It is a long and arduous undertaking.

That summer, I was eager to compare what was now happening in communities where I had once encountered apathy and despair. Not far from New Delhi is the village of Alipore, where, in October, 1952, Mr. Nehru officially inaugurated India's now famous Community Development Program. I decided to pay a visit to that village.

As the residents tell the story of that momentous day, Pandit Nehru found the people in a holiday mood. The lanes through which he was to pass were festooned with flags and flowers. High officials were on hand to welcome their distinguished guest and escort him to the platform.

Mr. Nehru looked out over the faces of thousands who had walked long distances in the heat to listen to their Prime Minister. He regarded his expectant audience with some dismay. Then, he turned to the master of ceremonies and declared: "I didn't come here to make a speech."

"But, sir, the programs are printed. They are expecting it of you."

"Then, all right," replied the Prime Minister.

After sitting impatiently through the long introductions, he stood up and delivered what his friends believe to be the shortest speech of his career: "Ladies and gentlemen: The time for speechmaking is over. We have arrived at the time for toil and sweat. As long as there are tears and suffering, our work will see no end."

Suddenly, while the crowd looked on open-mouthed, Mr. Nehru left the platform, moved swiftly down the steps, and strode over to a knot of workmen who had come to hear him speak. He took a shovel from one of them and began to dig.

With that spontaneous gesture, the greatest war on poverty ever to be waged in the name of democracy was declared. Eleven years later, I was in this same village, looking at the results of the inspiring effort which had taken place in the meantime. They were impressive.

In the center of the village was a brick community center, neatly landscaped, which I learned had been built by the villagers themselves. Nearby was a new school attended by most of the children in the village. Electric lights had begun to make their appearance. Homes were neat. Here and there were kitchen gardens, and pens of thriving chickens. Beyond the confines of the village was a network of irrigation canals.

The water and electricity, I was informed, came from a dam built with the aid and assistance of U.S. engineers loaned under Point Four. The chickens were in good health because of a balanced feeding program and a new type of serum instrumental in stamping out plague (New Castle disease) which a Point Four veterinarian had helped to develop.

Even more important was the change in the spirit of the people. The villagers of Alipore were happy and proud. They went about their work, not with listless despair, but with hope and confidence in the future.

I reached Korea about the time that there was much criticism of foreign aid being published in our local papers. Many of us had heard much of the blunders made there in the name of foreign aid—of the laundromats that went unattended because there was no water, and of a flour mill built in a district where there was no wheat, of theft of materials, and embezzlement on the part of some local officers.

But we had learned nothing of a successful enterprise. I was astonished, therefore, when I was shown a thriving factory in the suburbs of Seoul, a factory launched with foreign aid funds where 300,000 bicycles had been produced in 1962, and 850 small three-wheeled motor trucks had been built for service in the narrow streets.

In Egypt, I encountered two projects typical of foreign aid endeavors in that they were almost impossible to evaluate.

Back in 1952, I had been impressed by a project sixteen miles from Cairo where Point Four workers were helping to develop a deeply rooted drought-resistant pasture grass that would be suitable for cows, goats, and camels. It was a low-cost project that appeared to fill a need, and the people appreciated it. On my 1963 visit, I was surprised to learn that it had been abandoned. What surprised me even more was that I was unable to find out why.

In the mid-1950's, a foreign aid official in Egypt was inspired to want to help improve the poultry flocks of the fellahs. In cooperation with a private agency, 18,000 baby chicks were dispatched in a single planeload. This gave rise to considerable criticism. Only meager facilities were available to receive the new arrivals in such large number. Many died. Many more fell sick. Egyptian agriculturists complained angrily that new diseases had been introduced within their borders.

Yet, as I toured villages in 1963, I saw signs of strong healthy flocks, some of which must have come from these original chicks. Perhaps, with hindsight, one could say that it might have been done better. But could one say that it should not have been done at all?

Just before I left Egypt, I met a man dressed in the long robe of the Egyptian farmer, hard at work on his two and one-quarter acres, awarded to him under the new land reclamation program which foreign aid had assisted.

With a heavy spade, he was breaking up clods. His two boys were helping him by breaking up the smaller clods with clubs. His wife was leveling the ground with a hoe.

"How does it feel to be working your own land?" I asked him.

"Now it's like sun-up all day," he said as he went on pounding. "We do not feel tired any more."

Those few heartfelt words were more eloquent to me than volumes of official reports.

There were other gratifying results. In many places I saw advances in the war against malaria, often called "the tropical man's worst killer." In Jordan, for example, 15,000 cases in 1954 had been reduced to 50 by 1962. In the Philippines, where AID had granted $5 million for DDT, spraying equipment, and technical services, the annual total of cases dropped from 2 million to 30,000 within 10 years.

In Thailand, efforts to free the country from dependence on the single crop, rice, were paying off. AID technicians introduced seed corn from Guatemala, where the climate was similar, and it was doing well. Corn production had been increased by thirty-fold, and corn was on its way to being a major crop. Also under AID sponsorship, citrus trees had been brought in from Formosa. By 1962, more than 100,000 improved citrus trees were growing in newly established orchards.

However, I noticed a change of atmosphere in various countries which made me uneasy. I looked in vain for people such as those I had met on my earlier visit: for a Hans Kardell, standing against his jeep on a hot summer night in the village square while he discoursed on seeds; or a Frank Pinder, "the walking American" hustling along the jungle trail from one African village to another; or Henry Botch, relentlessly pursuing the hoards of rats through Iraq granaries with poison gas and pellets; or a radiant Dr. Flemmie Kittrell, cajoling the village headman into allowing her and her students to build a smokeless stove as a demonstration.

Instead, an undue proportion of AID men, some former shirt-sleeved county agents from the U.S., were behind desks, shuffling reports and various papers. I had a feeling that the foreign aid program had been quarantined from the people —into the embassy compound and confined there. Why?

In Washington, the higher echelons speak of this as the new "turn around," that things were done in a professional way now, government-to-government, with sums of money loaned and contracts to bring about change. But I felt, and still feel, that we have strayed from the original path and badly need to get back, that it is this very matter in which much of the current dissatisfaction lies.

In 1775, we began a revolution. That revolution, identical in spirit, although perhaps taking a different form, has by now spread over the world. Ours was first political, then industrial, then agricultural. We could take on one phase at a time.

Other countries must undertake their revolutions all at once, not only in the political and economic spheres, but in such matters as public health, population control, food production, and education. Foreign aid is the mechanism by which we can extend our help to them.

In the late autumn of 1963, when I returned from my

latest journey among the deprived peoples of the world, I was under no illusions that foreign aid had done anything like the job that had been hoped for, or that all was well. The most dewy-eyed idealist could scarcely avoid seeing that there had been much waste and poor judgment, that expectations had not been realized. Clearly, we had oversold both to ourselves and to striving peoples the idea of "American know-how."

Yet, one had also seen cause for pride and reason for hope, and that however imperfect our efforts, the need was greater than ever. In view of this, I was shocked by the expressions I heard as soon as the plane landed.

"End it all!"

"What are we getting out of it?"

"We can't carry the world on our shoulders."

Hardheaded businessmen declared we must be "realistic." Here was a word whose full meaning I felt was being overlooked. Men in industry well know that profits are not made without investment, often indeed only at great risk.

Something was very wrong, for it is not like Americans to give up because the first planting has failed to produce a bumper crop. The apparent disappointment at home was not in keeping with the idealism of a dozen years ago. But I could not believe that the true American spirit was in retreat. There was evidence to the contrary.

On June 2, 1960, the National Council of Churches declared its view: "To help to improve the standards of life for our fellow men is a privilege the United States shares, not a benefit it confers."

Pope John's pronouncement in his 1961 Encyclical was widely quoted and frequently cited by men of all faiths: "Communities enjoying an abundance of material goods are not to remain indifferent to those political communities whose citizens suffer from poverty, misery, and hunger."

Robert Theobald, consultant on economics, spoke for a large number of our best thinkers when he warned in the *International Development Review,* "Worldwide poverty is not only morally wrong but highly dangerous."

In the midst of intense feelings, some reasonable questions were being raised. Among them were these:

Is the amount we spend on foreign aid placing an undue burden on our economy?

Is foreign aid producing the kind of result taxpayers have a right to expect?

Has a program which combines both military and economic aid proved to be feasible?

If our place in history summons us to share some of the problems of emerging nations, how can this be accomplished with greater efficiency?

Is foreign aid, as currently administered, leading toward national security and a constructive end to the cold war?

It is hard for us to realize, but we are, in fact, engaged in a new kind of war, a war against hunger. Not only are a few allies involved, but all the nations of the earth, against an enemy that maims and kills more people each year than any war in history.

We are at a critical moment in the greatest endeavor in the history of mankind. If we falter now, if we choose to withdraw to our own pleasant homes, to our affluence, to avert our eyes from the poor and the hungry—the human side of world economic development—then all too soon the view from our thermopane window will be darkened by the accusing faces of peoples and nations who challenge our right to the privileges which we have come to accept as matter-of-course.

Let us now trace the course by which foreign aid has come to its present critical situation.

2

HOW DID WE GET HERE?

MANY AMERICANS with whom I have discussed foreign aid look upon it as a concept of modern times which came into being hard on the heels of World War II.

This view leads them to regard the program as one without roots or precedent, and therefore embodying a philosophy that is both dubious and suspect. But the actual fact is that our tradition of aid to other peoples runs like a continuous thread through our nation's history, from the earliest days of the Republic.

On a bleak winter day in 1794, several thousand seaweary soldiers and planters, the remnant of a small French colony in Haiti (Santo Domingo), abandoned their ramshackle ships and scrambled ashore near Baltimore. They had held out as long as they could against the Spanish and British who were bent on seizing the island. When the revolution boiled over, those who could do so had fled to the American mainland.

The citizens of Baltimore who were faced with caring for these unfortunate refugees called upon Congress for help.

Congress moved swiftly, though with caution, and appropriated $15,000 for the welfare of "such of the inhabitants of Saint Domingo, resident within the United States, as shall be found in need of support." The Chief Executive was authorized to draw upon this sum, and to direct its distribution "in such manner as shall, in the opinion of the President, appear most conducive to the humane purpose of this Act."

A few years later, in 1812, Venezuela was deep in her struggle for independence from Spain, when, on Holy Thursday, March 12, a devastating earthquake left the city of Caracas in ruins. Cathedrals collapsed upon worshipers who had gathered to pray. In all, some 20,000 lives were lost.*

Alexander Scott, our special representative to Venezuela, happened to be home in the United States at the time. Reporting to James Monroe, then Secretary of State, he suggested:

> Under these circumstances the Government might feel disposed to indulge our native feelings of generosity in administering to the wants of the unhappy sufferers. . . . Such an act of philanthropy, besides adding to the lustre of the American character, would be popular with the people of that country; it would succor the distressed and comfort the afflicted, being not less noble and magnanimous among the nations than among individuals.

Discussion in Congress was exhaustive. In the end, $50,000 was appropriated for the purchase of "such provisions as the President shall deem advisable, and to render the same in the name of the Government of the United States to that of Venezuela, for the relief of the citizens who have suffered from the late earthquake." Supplies consisting of 4,272 barrels of flour and 2,728 bushels of corn were bought and shipped at a cost of $47,840.

Representative John Rhea, who introduced the resolution, said he was "activated by regard for the interests of

* E. Taylor Parks, *Foreign Service Journal,* U.S. Department of State, July, 1962.

the United States which peculiarly require us to cultivate amity with the South American Provinces."

Down through the years other similar situations have arisen. Just at the close of the century, on March 3, 1899, Congress voted $100,000 to Cuba, thus compensating that country to some extent for the suffering and losses caused by the Spanish-American War.

Following the outbreak of World War I, in August, 1914, Herbert Hoover helped to form the Commission for Relief in Belgium. The Commission was supported by grants from Britain, France, and the United States. The British allowed the passage of food, clothing, and medicines through the allied blockade. The Germans gave permission for the distribution of these supplies to more than 10 million distressed people in Belgium and northern France. Under Mr. Hoover's direction, the Commission expended nearly $1 billion.

When the United States entered the war in April, 1917, President Wilson appointed Mr. Hoover as head of the U.S. Food Administration. During the year 1919 alone, this agency dispatched 18.5 million tons of food to the Allies and to the famine areas of Europe, spent $3.25 billion in relief funds, and distributed some 23 million tons of clothing and medicines as our contribution toward rehabilitating war-torn countries.

Mr. Hoover later set up a relief organization that distributed voluntary gifts to the extent of $250 million for the aid of people in Europe, extending as far as Armenia and Russia.

Again, after the end of World War II, when the nations of Greece and Turkey were about to collapse, President Truman requested $400 million which Congress granted for "commodities, supplies, and needed equipment." (This was in advance of the Marshall Plan.)

In all these instances, Congress assumed no responsibility beyond the appropriation of grants of money. It was only in the face of devastation following World War II that the American people reached the decision to engage systematically in foreign aid as a matter of national policy.

Europe was a shambles. Factories, bombed out, were silent. Homes were destroyed. Cities were dark for lack of electric power. Farmers, for the lack of livestock, seed, or implements, were unable to produce. The strictest rationing failed to prevent inflation. People already grieved by the loss of their loved ones were further bowed down by poverty and want not of their own making. The threat of Communist takeover to exploit the widespread discontent was imminent.

The Marshall Plan and ECA

There were both humanitarian and economic reasons for our extension of assistance to Europe. From an economic standpoint, the United States had prospered while Europe suffered. Our shores had been spared the physical destruction of war which the Continent and England had endured. Sales of goods and war matériel had greatly strengthened our gold reserve.

On June 15, 1947, General George C. Marshall, then Secretary of State, delivered an eventful commencement address at Harvard University. He chose the occasion to make public his carefully deliberated views on the problems of European recovery and our responsibility.

> The people of this country are distant from the troubled areas of the earth. It is hard for them to comprehend the plight and subsequent reactions of long-suffering peoples and the effect of these reactions on their governments and our efforts to promote peace in the world.
>
> The truth of the matter is that Europe's requirements for the next three or four years, of food and other essential products, principally from America, are so much greater than her ability to pay that she must have substantial additional help or face economic, social, and political deterioration. It is logical that the United States should do whatever it is able to do to assist the return of normal economic health in the world. Without this, there can be no political stability, and no assured peace.
>
> Our policy is directed not against any country or doctrine, but against hunger, poverty, desperation, and chaos. With foresight and a willingness on the part of our people to face up

to the vast responsibility which history has clearly placed upon our country, the difficulties I have outlined can and will be overcome.

It was thought that the Marshall proposal might cost the United States as much as $17 billion, distributed over a four or five year period. Realizing that some aid to war-torn Europe was essential, many lawmakers, editors, and other molders of public opinion, accepted the idea at once. Others viewed the plan with skepticism. In the long history of nations, it was still a new idea for one country voluntarily to hand over $5 billion a year to other countries.

Senator Arthur Vandenberg, then Chairman of the Foreign Relations Committee, observed: "No administration would dare to come to the Senate with such a proposal." Early opinion polls revealed a large segment of the public was opposed to the suggestion.

Congress clearly saw the two alternatives: Either it must go to work to assure the speedy economic recovery of Europe, or it must face the consequences of the Continent's economic collapse.

However, in drafting legislation to aid Europe, Congress set up the strictest of guidelines. Countries wishing to participate were required to make specific commitments regarding lower trade barriers, improved production goals, and business methods.

Some weren't eager to accept aid on these terms. Pride and fear of political involvement were among the principal reasons for their caution. Winston Churchill suggested that military aid might be preferable. But in spite of objections, sixteen nations ultimately joined in what was to be known as the Marshall Plan for European Recovery.

The Act was passed by Congress in April, 1948. The Economic Cooperation Administration (ECA) was set up to put the new act into effect. During the first fifteen months, Congress appropriated $5.6 billion for its implementation.

The countries of Europe possessed the three ingredients for rapid recovery: technical skill, administrative ability, and the will to succeed.

Within months smoke was rising once more from factory chimneys. Once again lines of workers moved through the gates. With a modernized industrial plant, France and Western Germany in particular were on their way to achieving a greater economic vitality than they had enjoyed before. Our $17 billion investment, prudently applied over the years 1948–52 had perhaps been the decisive factor in rescuing Europe from the brink of collapse.

Point Four Is Born

Four years after the war in the Pacific ended, Chiang Kai-shek was in Nanking to draft terms of cease-fire and surrender which would be acceptable to the Communist armies. He had previously agreed to leave China and go to Formosa. All that remained was to settle on conditions that would assure his safety en route.

In New Delhi, delegates from Asian countries met to ask the United Nations to request that the Netherlands forthwith extend full independence to Indonesia. France was in the midst of her fruitless struggle to keep the lid down in Indochina.

In the Philippines, the hukbalahap movement was gathering momentum. The huks had emerged during the Japanese occupation as a guerrilla force. At the close of the war, they turned on the landlords in an effort to bring about land reform by force. Backed by a strong Communist Party, the huks were bent on overthrowing the wobbly Quirino government.

Their attitude was typical of so many in Asian countries who, hoping for a better life at the close of the war, had found only continued poverty and misery. These people felt that they had nothing to lose by revolution. As a huk leader in Luzon remarked to a missionary friend of mine: "If you're already sleeping on the floor, you can't fall out of bed."

In India, two years of independence had not brought the sweeping reforms that students and impatient political leaders were demanding overnight. Nearly every village had its

Communist agents who were busy stirring up unrest. In Calcutta and other cities, the hungry were rioting for food.

On August 16, 1947, the day after India celebrated her independence, Mahatma Gandhi received a cabled request from an American publisher to this effect: "Kindly give us a 2,000 word statement on 'Our New Rights Under Independence.' Honorarium, $5,000."

Gandhi smiled as he put the cablegram aside. Then he penciled his reply: "We have no rights. Only new duties."

In Iran, the peasant laborers were in open revolt. Syria, Turkey, and Greece were politically embroiled, both internally and externally. Russia, hungry for access to the sea on the south, was putting heavy pressure on her neighbors.

At this time, the U.N. census put the population of the so-called underdeveloped countries at more than 1.5 billion.

Such was roughly the state of the world on the eve of Inauguration Day, January 20, 1949. The lights burned late in the White House; President Truman was putting the final touches on his inaugural address.

"I had about three or four hours' sleep that night," he told several of us some years later. "The weather forecast was mighty gloomy, but I don't take much stock in forecasts of any kind, as you know. Anyway, the day dawned clear, and I was ready."

At noon, bareheaded, he stepped out into the biting wind before a shivering audience of some 120,000. Most people were familiar with the look of determination so characteristic of this man who had defied the experts by winning an election they had been certain he would lose. Now, in the chill air and brilliant sunshine, his expression reflected not only the gravity which the occasion called for, but the manifestation of some inner strength.

Forthrightly, with deliberation, he delivered his address, making four specific points:

> First: We will continue our unfaltering support of the United Nations and related agencies.
>
> Second: We will continue programs for European recovery.

> Third: We will strengthen the freedom-loving nations against aggression.

Then the President hesitated. He was about to propose an extraordinary departure in American foreign policy. He said:

> Fourth: We must embark on a bold new program for making the benefits of our scientific advances and industrial progress available for the improvement and growth of underdeveloped areas.

Thus came into being that milestone in our history which was to be known as Point Four. The remainder of his address was devoted to the explanation and unfolding of this great dream. Some of the more telling points he made at that time I quote here as a reminder of original aims which may have become lost in today's murky confusion.

> More than half the people of the world are living in conditions approaching misery. Their food is inadequate. They are victims of disease. Their economic life is primitive and stagnant. Their poverty is a handicap and a threat both to them and to the more prosperous areas. . . .
>
> I believe that we should make available to peace-loving peoples the benefits of our technical knowledge in order to help them realize their aspirations for a better life. Our aim should be to help the free peoples of the world, through their own efforts, to produce more food, more clothing, more materials for housing, and more mechanical power to lighten their burdens. . . .
>
> We invite other countries to pool their technological resources in the undertaking. This should be a cooperative enterprise in which all nations work together through the United Nations and its specialized agencies wherever practicable. It must be a world-wide effort for the achievement of peace, plenty, and freedom. . . .
>
> Only by helping the least fortunate of its members to help themselves can the human family achieve the decent, satisfying life that is the right of all people.

In closing, the President said, "Events have brought American democracy to new influence, new responsibilities.

With faith in God we can advance toward a world where man's freedom is secure." A shivering but enthusiastic audience thundered its applause.

Reactions from Congress were cautious. Senator Homer Ferguson observed: "We must be careful of trying to buy peace with the taxpayers' dollars." Senator James Byrd did not view the plan "as wise or practical." It was the opinion of Senator Arthur Vandenberg that "existing international plans should be perfected before new ones are begun."

Senator Jacob Javits was one of the few who expressed enthusiasm. He said: "The proposal for the extension of technological help to other democratic nations represents one of the most fruitful concepts for future development of the world and for resisting Communistic influences."

In Moscow, Joseph Stalin derided the plan as "a new design for extending imperialism." The Communist Daily Worker dismissed it as, "a gibe against Communism. He [President Truman] speaks for a country which waxed fat out of the war and with not a bomb on its territory."

But David Owen, then Assistant Secretary General of the United Nations, hailed Point Four as "the most encouraging news I have heard since I joined the organization." And the far-off *Hindustan Times* exulted: "Point Four shot new hope into the veins of a striving but languishing world."

British papers reacted with praise. *The London Times* said: "It showed a new sense of American responsibility." *The London Telegraph:* "We are delighted to see the emphasis laid on world purposes." To *The Financial Times* it was "evidence of the distance America has traveled in the last few years."

In Italy, *Giornalia d'Italia* called the speech "one of the noblest documents of humanity."

In its lead editorial for January 21, 1949, *The New York Times* said of Point Four:

> It was a call to dedication for the democratic spirit. . . . It left us a new vision of freedom, of plenty, of human dignity, of generous sharing. . . . It was democracy looking homeward

across a continent, but also looking outward across a world in which democracy will never again be impotent or ashamed.

At a press conference six days after the inaugural address, a reporter bluntly asked the President: "Was this a studied proposal or was it, as some are saying, just a speech?"

President Truman seized the opportunity to clarify a question in the minds of many. He stated:

> The original idea of Point Four has been in my mind and in the minds of my government associates for the last two or three years, ever since the Marshall Plan and aid to Greece and Turkey. I spend much time going over that globe back there trying to figure out ways to make peace in the world. It is new because unlike our previous philanthropies it is not focused toward any particular country or emergency.

Debate over Point Four continued in Congress throughout 1949. There were questions to which no one had the answers. How long would such a program take? What would it cost? Which of the hundred or more underdeveloped countries should be helped? How could we avoid appearing to favor one country to the neglect of others?

The Secretary of State, Dean Acheson, defended Point Four at a meeting of the Senate Committee on Foreign Relations. "I know of no better investment for the American people at this time," he declared.

Secretary of Agriculture, Charles Brannan, claimed: "Technical assistance in agriculture will bring back a hundredfold whatever we invest."

But the winter months passed, with no decisive action taken by Congress.

Technical Cooperation Administration (TCA)

At last, in May, 1950, the Act for International Development was passed. Under it, the President delegated his authority to the State Department. From that day on, responsibility for the program was assigned to Under Secretary of State Willard L. Thorp.

On September 6, 1950, Congress put through its first appropriation, $34.5 million for the program. Of this sum, $12 million was earmarked for foreign aid to be spent through the United Nations Special Fund.

In the office of Dr. Henry Garland Bennett, president of the Oklahoma State University at Stillwater, the telephone rang. It was October 30. Willard Thorp was on the line.

"I'm calling on behalf of President Truman," said Thorp. "He would like you to head up the new Point Four program. Would you be willing?"

"Would I be willing! Of course! When does he want me?"

"Now. Right away."

Within hours, Dr. Bennett was making arrangements for his departure to take on the responsibilities of the Technical Cooperation Administration, soon to be known as TCA.

In background and experience, he was well-suited to the job. Born on a farm in Arkansas, he had taught in a one-room country school, had later become a county superintendent, and finally had been picked for Oklahoma State University. He had also served, after World War II, as U.S. representative on a commission for feeding war-ravaged Europe.

White-haired, tall, and ruddy-faced, Bennett was imposing in manner. He walked with a vigorous stride. His friendly, penetrating eyes and deliberate, kindly voice instilled confidence wherever he went. An enthusiast, he was already known for his phrase: "Let's go do it!"

Dr. Bennett brought not only his natural gifts to the new program, but considerable experience and skill as an educator, an agriculturist, and a statesman.

Very soon he contributed his own memorable definition of Point Four: *"Simple, down-to-earth, self-help to assist other peoples to increase their food production, better their health conditions, and improve their educational system* [italics added]."

I have often thought how many frustrations and disappointments might have been avoided if that concept had been adhered to more closely.

When the new Administrator reached Washington, he found the place already yeasting with grandiose ideas. The atmosphere was exuberant with the gratifying success achieved by the Marshall Plan. TCA officials were impatient for "quick and massive action."

The vast difference between restoring war-torn Europe and the immense difficulties of extending similar aid to underdeveloped countries had not yet become evident. In Europe, institutions for the handling of credit for banking, marketing, and transportation were long established and highly developed. There was no shortage of seasoned managerial talent. Skilled workmen were ready to man the machines as soon as they could be provided.

Conditions in the countries to which we now proposed to extend aid were in marked contrast to those of Western Europe. The task here would entail not so much the restoration of a bruised economy in essence very much like our own, but rather, the building of a new structure from the ground up.

We now had to work with peoples imbued with new hope and impatience, with new awareness, yet skeptical. Though eager to rise, their attitudes had been shaped by living for generations under oppression in regions of exhausted soil and inadequate water supply. They were handicapped by the eagerness to pour in people, materials, and funds faster than they could be put to work.

Within six months after Congress had passed the budget for Point Four, 350 technicians were sent to 27 countries in Asia, Africa, and Latin America. Over 100 projects had been launched; more than 250 trainees from other lands had been brought to the United States. The American people, generous by nature and anxious for speedy results, were crying: "Appropriate more money! Send more technicians!"

In October, 1951, Dr. Bennett invited a number of leaders in church and government circles to meet with him in Philadelphia. His purpose was to discover ways through which these two groups might work together more effectively to advance the Point Four program.

He said to us: "The slow, studied approach—that is the application of technical skill and the capital necessary to bring about success in such an enterprise—is being abandoned. Too many people and too much money behind Point Four, at this stage, are a hindrance."

Sitting across the heavy oak table from us in the Philadelphia hotel room, Dr. Bennett, usually so serene and so sure of himself, seemed perplexed, even baffled.

"We've too many cooks in Washington," he sighed. "The broth is being spoiled. Sometimes I'm not even sure who is my boss. The curtain goes up and comes down again before we've had time to finish anything. They keep calling for reports—endless reports—paper plans and more paper plans. Why, we're developing a bureau before we've got a program."

By this time, he told us, the program was plunging ahead, swept along by its own momentum. Bureaucracy burgeoned. Agriculturists, engineers, businessmen, teachers, and social workers were eager for a chance to go abroad. Selection was difficult because few of the applicants could be given any idea of what would be expected of them. Only a handful had any overseas experience; there was no orientation or special training. Separate departments for recruiting and assignment to host countries sprang up overnight. But there were no clear lines of authority. As Dr. Bennett described the situation: "No one individual can direct the course of such a Hydra-headed creature."

Then, almost prophetically, he added: "We Americans like to measure performance by the number of people on the payroll, the amount of money allocated. Personally, I cannot regard this sort of forced feeding as judicious."

It was not long after the Philadelphia conference that Dr. Bennett took off for the Near East on an extended field trip. On the afternoon of December 23, 1951, the plane carrying the Administrator and eight of his associates to Teheran crashed in a dense fog. All on board were killed. Foreign aid, barely getting under way, suffered a staggering blow.

President Truman called in Stanley Andrews, then Director of the Office of Foreign Agricultural Relations in the Department of Agriculture, to take over, pro tem. In the meantime, the search for a permanent administrator got under way.

Later, Stanley Andrews told how he came to be chosen to succeed Dr. Bennett. "Point Four was only a year old," he said, "but it was already in high gear. Almost everyone was new on the job, loose ends all over the place. Only Henry knew the score. Suddenly he was gone. I was asked to go over and hold things together. For three months I commuted back and forth between the two offices.

"Then, one morning my secretary rushed in, breathless, and said: 'The White House wants you.'

"I picked up the phone. It was Mr. Dawson, President Truman's assistant. 'The boss wants to see you,' he said.

" 'Now what have I done?'

" 'It's about Point Four.'

"Minutes later I was ushered into the President's office. In my Arkansas drawl, I mumbled something like, 'I hear you want to see me.' The President squared around.

" 'Well, three of my cabinet were just here. They tell me you're the man to run Point Four.'

"I stammered: 'I can think of at least a dozen men who could run that better than I. Why pick an Arkansas apple knocker?'

"Then the President became serious. He replied: 'You know, if I'm remembered for anything fifty years from now, it will probably be because my name was connected with Point Four. I want you to take over the job. Run it like it was your own. If you hit any tough decisions you know my telephone number. Call me up. I'll make them for you.'

"The President put out his hand and I was off."

In spite of his own modest estimate, Stanley Andrews, like Henry Bennett before him, was well qualified for the job. Reared on a Missouri farm, he later held a series of influential government posts related to world agriculture as consultant on international food supply problems. He served TCA well for nineteen months.

By the end of 1954, there were 3,010 technical experts on

the job in 43 countries. Of these, 850 had been assigned to Latin America; 1,100 to the Near East and North Africa; and 1,060 to Southeast Asia. They were roughly apportioned as follows: 40 per cent for agriculture; 25 per cent for industry; 25 per cent for health and education; 10 per cent for miscellaneous enterprises.

Many of the technicians arrived on the scene before the host governments were able to make any plans for their effective use. There was constant coming and going. Most of the appointments were for no more than one or two years, many for only a month or several weeks. Planes carrying new hands passed those bearing workers who were already returning home. All these factors multiplied administrative troubles at both ends.

Complications were beginning to pile up. At this juncture of the program, as today, public opinion was sinking to a low ebb. Had too much been attempted too fast? Confusion reigned; many and serious bottlenecks had developed. Rivalries and jealousies began to show up among the different groups of U.S. workers overseas.

But there was a bright side. I went to Washington at a time when charges of bureaucracy, waste, and extravagance filled the air. I encountered any number of able and conscientious executives struggling to find solutions to complex problems. But it was out in the field, in spite of the disenchantment, that one saw much of value being accomplished.

It is true that in the airport cities, the hotels were choked with Point Four technicians, restlessly and uselessly awaiting assignment while their children romped through lobbies, and bored wives went window-shopping.

But out in the countryside I met specialists—teachers, county agents, public health experts—quietly, and selflessly, hard at work on their jobs. Such people, working with tact, sympathy, and understanding, were endearing themselves to local officers and villagers in at least forty countries. Their achievements may be brought into sharper focus by citing case histories of just a few of them.

In 1953, I was traveling from Coimbatore to Bangalore

when I ran into Horace Holmes, an old friend of mine who had just been appointed director of agriculture for TCA in India. His was the familiar story—Point Four people piling into New Delhi before the Indian Government could find anything constructive for them to do. He expressed his exasperation.

Then he said: "Why don't you go look up Hans Kardell? He'll give you another side of the picture, and he'll give it to you straight, because he's a straight shooter."

Late one afternoon several days later, my bus dropped me on the edge of the little village of Murabad. The smoke curling up from the thatched-roof houses, laden with pungent smells, told me that the housewives were busy cooking the evening meal.

Under a spreading neem tree in the village square stood a crowd of about 150 farmers, all quiet and intent. The focus of their attention was a fair-haired man of medium height who stood leaning against a cart, his khaki shirt open at the neck, speaking to them in energy-charged, earnest sentences.

"If millet is your main crop, sometimes fertilizer *will* help. . . . But you've got to have more water. . . . How good is your seed, anyway?"

After each few bullet-like words, he stopped. A man at his side who might have been the village school teacher repeated them in Hindi, like a litany, like a chant. No doubt about it, this man had to be Hans Kardell.

"Incidentally," Kardell was saying, "where do you go when you want to borrow money? And how much do you have to pay for it?"

The crowd rumbled. He had touched a sensitive chord.

So it went. Half an hour later, when he had finished, the farmers surged around him. They were entreating him to come back, and to come back soon.

The translator introduced himself to me.

"Mr. Kardell belongs to us," he said with a proprietary air. "I hope I am of help to him. I tell him what the farmers say. I tell them what he suggests they do."

I rode back with Hans Kardell to Bangalore in his

jeep, and had dinner with the family in their small apartment. From what he told me about his early life, it had eminently fitted him for his present job. A Michigan farm boy of Danish parentage, he paid his way through college by working as a farm laborer; then he had served low income farmers as a county agricultural agent for eighteen years. He had brought to his present job three invaluable assets: a broad, firsthand knowledge of farming, a fund of common sense, and genuine admiration for the people among whom he worked.

"I want to see this thing get off the ground," he said. "Otherwise I wouldn't be here. But there's a lot we've got to consider besides farming. Take one thing—how'd *you* like to be a citizen of a poor country, to be on the receiving end and have to listen to somebody who's come out to tell you the *right* way to do it? I ask myself such questions every day. Maybe they already know what's best but lack the tools and other supplies.

"One other thing—they can't afford to have us make any mistakes. Oh, we can make them, and go home, and forget. They have to live with them. We'd better know what we're doing—or shut up."

Recently I came across a couple of lines I wrote in my fieldbook after I got home that night: "If Point Four can have at least one Hans Kardell on every team, its usefulness will be assured." I still stand on that.

Hans Kardell has since died. But he has left behind him a wealth of good will and a matrix for future work of incalculable value.

A few weeks later, I was in a small village in western India having tea with the district magistrate, when, to my astonishment, I thought I heard the words "village queen" fall from his lips.

"Did I understand you correctly?" I asked.

"Oh, that's just the affectionate title by which she is best known among the women of our villages. Her real name is Dr. Kittrell, and I believe she was dean of home economics at your own Howard University?" The magistrate went on to explain that Dr. Kittrell had been sent to open a similar home economics department at Baroda University, but kept insisting that she and the students go out into the villages.

She used to say: " 'You can't teach home economics unless you know what things are like in the homes.' "

He clasped his hands on his polished teakwood desk and looked at me.

"Can you imagine what that means to us? For a visiting professor to do something like that?

"Here's a story that is typical," he went on. "She had come upon the idea of a simple little stove—something anybody could make—out of mud and home-baked bricks, with a tile chimney to carry the smoke out of the room. The idea was that it would generate more heat with less fuel—and you know how scarce fuel is around here. Local workers had tried to introduce the stove but without success. So Dr. Kittrell decided to put the prestige of her office behind it.

"She and her students visited a neighboring village to try to introduce this novel way of building a stove. Knowing her protocol, she went first to the headman. But he would have none of it.

"But Dr. Kittrell did not leave. The next morning she approached the headman again. Her students had found an abandoned shack outside the village. Would he mind if they built a demonstration stove there? The headman could hardly refuse.

"So the Dean and her students built the stove while a handful of housewives looked on. A few of them went home to try the plan themselves. Others began to imitate them. The notion spread.

"Several months passed. A few days before Dr. Kittrell was to leave for America, she received from the headman's wife an invitation to tea. Shyly, the wife explained that the tea had been brewed on a stove she had made herself, according to the plan. The headman himself, now completely won over, showed his appreciation by placing a garland of flowers about Dr. Kittrell, saying, 'You are now the queen of our village.' "

When I stopped off in Burma in 1958, they were still

talking about Otto Hunerwadel who had been sent out from Tennessee where he had been an extension agent, and about his wife, and his red jeep.

Otto arrived in the early 1950's. He didn't waste any time around the AID head office in Rangoon. He piled into his red jeep, along with Mrs. H. and an interpreter, and took off. For a while they just roved around, talked with the villagers, made notes of what they saw, and thought of ways to do things better.

Hunerwadel came on some farmers broadcasting their millet and alfalfa seed. He explained the advantage of planting in rows. He sent back home for some seed that did better in that climate. He had some improved corn seed sent out from Tennessee. That did well.

Mrs. H. was surprised when she saw the women trying to sweep with flimsy grass brushes. Otto ordered some broom corn seed. That thrived too. The next year, he and several young men were making good sturdy brooms out of it. He saw that the hoes weren't much good because they were made out of soft, malleable iron. It was not easy to persuade the blacksmith to make a blade out of tempered steel, but he finally obliged.

True, Otto might be criticized for spending too much of his time on too few people, too small details. But he was buying experience; he was earning the eventual right to speak to Burmese government officers.

While Otto was busy in the fields, Mrs. H., who had a home economics background, was busy on her own, making friends with the women. She worked with them in making comfortable mattresses and cushions with the kapok that grew outside their doors, and taught them how to preserve fruits and vegetables. Women came from miles around to attend her classes in nutrition.

At the time Otto and Helen were working in Burma, conditions were pretty bad in that part of the country. Banditry was rife, and the red jeep was easy to spot. But no one ever bothered the Hunerwadels. The word had gone out.

In the mountains of Colombia, Latin America, Father

Francisco Medina was worried about the dilapidated houses of his parishioners. He had been working on this problem for years. The people had given him their minimum needs: three rooms with built-in kitchen and built-in beds, and an outside shelter for chickens and livestock. The only "hitch" was that the house could not cost them more than $250.

Father Medina arranged a meeting between the farmers and American officers in the region. Among them was William Olson, Point Four extension specialist. Olson helped to make bricks and mortar. Father Francisco organized the farmers who contributed the labor; the result was a community of sturdy, attractive homes at prices people could afford to pay.

These are only a few of the accomplishments of our "shirt-sleeve diplomats." They made no headlines. They worked quietly in remote parts of the world while words of criticism were flying on the front pages and in the halls of Congress. But they have left their mark.

In headquarters offices abroad and in Washington, the program was beginning to reap the whirlwind of headlong haste. As if this were not enough, a rapid series of changes in the governmental authority under which AID operated was compounding the confusion.

The Alphabetical Tangle

In 1951, the Korean crisis was coming to a head. The old Economic Cooperation Administration of Marshall Plan days was abolished; a new agency known as the Mutual Security Administration (MSA) was set up in its place, mainly to expedite the prosecution of the war.

The Technical Cooperation Administration continued as a separate agency under the State Department. Then, in 1953, TCA was combined with MSA to form a new agency known as the Foreign Operations Administration (FOA).

But FOA was short-lived. Within two years, it was abolished and its functions were transferred to an entirely new agency known as the International Cooperation Administration (ICA).

At last, in 1961, all the former agencies were merged into one in order to avoid duplication. This period is now referred to in Washington as the "year of the turn-around" for it was at that time that the name now in use for the agency, the Agency for International Development (AID) was evolved. This was the beginning of the current policy to contract for more short-term workers for a stipulated period only, and fewer career employees.

In the years since the beginning of Point Four, ten different directors have been in charge. Each sought to effect his own ideas for change. No other arena of government responsibility has been so frequently surveyed and changed. Eight Presidential committees have scrutinized it. Three administrations have completely overhauled it. This created grave doubt overseas as to our intentions.

Many of our more sensitive field men have seen the limitations of technology alone as an answer to deeply rooted problems. One returning specialist declared: "Illinois answers cannot be applied to Iranian problems."

Helping disadvantaged but proud peoples to raise their levels of living is proving to be a more exacting task than had been anticipated. It is one which calls not only for technology, but also for statesmanship of the highest order, for delicacy and understanding in human relations.

The past fourteen years in foreign aid add up to a confusion of good intentions, rapid changes, disillusionment, failures, and successes. Is it any wonder, then, that so many Americans have no clear idea of what the program is all about? Is it any wonder that so many statesmen and technicians in the developing countries are doubtful about our ability to comprehend and effectively help solve their problems?

There is confusion among American taxpayers about foreign aid's objectives; how much of it goes directly or indirectly for military purposes, how much for strictly humanitarian objectives? They have questions as to how it is administered, how decisions are reached. They are puzzled about the many changes in name. Naturally, they are skeptical.

Before exploring possible ways out of this dilemma, let us look at the basics of U.S. AID: how it is currently organized and administered.

3

U.S AID IN PROFILE

FOREIGN AID means various things to various people. Probably most of those who support it do so largely for humanitarian reasons. However, beyond this, people have special interests that must be considered.

To congressmen at work on our annual budget, foreign aid ultimately narrows down to the amount of money appropriated. As custodians of public funds, they must see that the proper amount is made available, that it is wisely used.

To the President, aid must be viewed broadly as an expression of our partnership with other nations in an effort to achieve peace, freedom, and security for all. "The rich nations must aid the poorer nations," said President Johnson before the United Nations Assembly in the summer of 1964.

To the Department of State, foreign aid is an instrument of foreign policy. It is believed, for example, that technical assistance or grants applied in strategic areas will assist nations in remaining free from subversion. Or grants of money and materials are sometimes used as inducement to bring a nation into political alignment with us.

To the military, foreign aid is considered as an extra rampart in our defense, a means for helping weak nations build up their strength. (Why military aid is involved and whether or not it should be considered as a part of the foreign aid program is explored more fully in Chapter 9.)

To the American businessman, foreign aid is a stimulus to employment and trade. Nearly 80 per cent of the funds used to buy aid materials are spent for American-made goods.

To the farmer, in addition to humanitarian concern, aid is a common sense way of sharing the abundance of food he produces.

To religious leaders, it is the fulfillment of moral and humanitarian responsibilities to those in need.

To statesmen of countries receiving aid, it is a help toward achieving economic growth and other reforms more rapidly than would be possible otherwise.

But most of all, to the deprived millions striving to rise from poverty and misery, foreign aid means hope for a better life. The late President Kennedy no doubt had this in mind when he said: "We do these things because they are right."

Such wide and varied interests make foreign aid difficult to administer, difficult for the average layman to understand fully.

Many changes have taken place in the years since Point Four was born. It has been administered by various authorities. It has been known by different names or sets of initials. For the sake of clarity, it may be helpful to sketch briefly the organization currently known as the Agency for International Development. It is now housed in the Department of State. AID's current Administrator, David E. Bell, ranks as an undersecretary. Four bureaus direct the program; their responsibility is distributed as follows: Europe and Africa, the Near East and South Asia, the Far East, and Latin America.

Each of these bureaus is headed by an assistant administrator with the rank of assistant secretary of state. Each bureau has its own staff, including specialists who deal with such matters as crops, land reform, cooperatives, public health, extension education, and research. Each of the bureaus also has separate officers and staff for each of the participating countries within its area.

In September, 1964, AID reported 2,926 employees in Washington, and 3,762 in 80 countries abroad.

Within each country, AID is organized as a mission under the U.S. Embassy. The director or head of each mission reports to the ambassador. In some African and Latin American countries where experience has been slight, missions assume responsibility for planning and administering their own programs within limits set down by the Department of State. In others, such as Nigeria, Pakistan, India, and the Philippines, most of our aid is channeled through programs already worked out by the host countries.

As of June 30, 1963, we had 3,504 technicians abroad, assigned to the following areas:

Near East and South Asia	948
Latin America	802
Far East	979
Africa	742
Europe	33

These men and women were engaged in different fields of work as follows:

Food and Agriculture	766
Education	358
Industry	337
Health and Sanitation	326
Transportation	324
Public Safety	200
Public Administration	158
Community Development	84

Labor	44
General and Miscellaneous	231
Technical Maintenance and Support	676

In discussions of foreign aid, the terms "plan," "program," and "project" are often used indiscriminately. The term "plan," as used in developing countries, and as used in this book is an over-all concept for social and economic growth. It is general in statement, broad in application. The term "program" is the means for carrying out the plan. It includes a series of activities such as efforts for literacy, extension education, seed production, malaria control, or farmers' credit. The "project" is any particular activity toward the execution of the program. It might be an adult class, the draining of a malarial swamp, construction of a road or use of fertilizers.

In brief, the over-all plan is achieved by means of the program, which, in turn, is implemented by a series of projects. Aid in a given country may range from a single project—a fertilizer factory, for example—to a complete program of public health, irrigation, teacher training, etc.

Types and Extent of Aid

Currently, 78 countries receive some form of United States aid. But more than 80 per cent of our expenditures are concentrated in 15 or 20 of them. The countries receiving the lion's share are: Greece, Turkey, Iran, Iraq, Afghanistan, Pakistan, India, Malaya, Thailand, South Vietnam, Laos, the Philippines, and Korea.

The amounts of aid allocated to different countries vary widely, and for good reason. Some nations possess both the experience and the personnel which enables them to make advantageous use of aid. Other countries, such as Korea and South Vietnam, receive more than what might be considered their normal share, for military reasons.

Economic aid is extended under four main categories: technical assistance, grants for development, aid by means of contracts with other agencies, and development loans. In actual practice, there is of necessity a good deal of overlapping, with several types of aid sometimes employed on the same project.

There are also subcategories such as fellowships for students and other trainees brought to the United States, guarantees to U.S. business firms undertaking risks abroad, and sharing the cost of surveys and advance studies with participating countries to determine the validity of proposed projects, or gifts, such as equipment to hospitals or schools.

Technical Assistance

This is the category of the aid program that makes it possible for our specialists to share knowledge and skills with citizens of other lands. In many underdeveloped countries, technology is in short supply, although these same countries may be further advanced than the West in certain of the arts and in philosophy.

Today, the term "technical assistance" is not limited to personnel, but has been broadened to include the funds and equipment necessary to enable specialists to function. How this principle operates in practice can perhaps be better understood by examining the case of Daniel Hayes, an educational specialist assigned to Liberia.

A native Kentuckian and a former country teacher with a Ph.D. from Cornell, Dr. Hayes soon learned that his job called for more than the working out of new curricula in a central office. "Anyone tackling this kind of work had better be prepared for the broadest interpretation of what it may include," he said. "In the hinterland—which is most of the country here—I found neither schools nor teachers on hand to implement a new curriculum, however good it might be. Before I could do much, I had to roll up my sleeves and lend a hand with the building of schoolhouses.

"We began by going into the bush, cutting the bamboo or palm poles and dragging them to the building site. We made the walls out of mud blocks. Wherever there was a window or a door, we lashed the poles together to make a frame. As a last step, the women gave the walls a smooth finish by plastering them, inside and out, with gray earth."

In the case of Dr. Hayes, his salary and working expenses are paid from funds allocated under technical assistance. He also has modest grants of money available with which to assist the people in buying sheet metal for roofing, door hinges or other hardware as might be needed. The young men and women in training to be teachers are assisted by aid through grants for that purpose. Here the use of several forms of aid in combination is not only desirable but essential.

Working in this way, aid becomes something more than an impersonal transaction between strangers—a warm and personal mutual undertaking. When Dr. Hayes visits a village school in the bush, the whole community is likely to turn out in jubilant welcome. The children blow lustily on their bamboo flutes; the young men thump their baboon skin drums.

Until 1954, malaria was Thailand's number one killer, taking nearly 30,000 lives a year. Millions afflicted by the debilitating illness were so weakened that they were unable to work. Thousands of fertile acres in which production was needed to feed the population could not be farmed at all because of the health hazard. I have visited villages where as many as half of the inhabitants were down with malaria.

Given such a disastrous situation, how can a combative campaign be organized effectively? Having observed a number of such campaigns, I have learned, contrary to general expectations, that this is a problem of extreme complexity.

Indeed, success might not be possible at all were it not for a point of vulnerability in the behavior of the mosquito. The insect invariably comes to rest for a moment in the interior wall of a building before administering the bite with which he infects his victim.

The spraying of interiors with DDT therefore becomes the first step in bringing malaria under control. But many other steps must also be taken: stagnant pools and various breeding places must be sprayed; medication for both prevention and cure must be given to thousands.

AID supplied seven experienced technicians; WHO, working in cooperation, provided a consulting specialist. Through AID funds, an army of 7,000 Thais was employed and trained, making it possible to carry out all phases of the operation on a broad front. Thai workers performed many specialized operations from mixing the chemicals to spraying the interiors in thousands of villages.

The war was waged over a period of nine years; for an antimalaria campaign to be successful, it must be continued year after year. The results were impressive. By 1963, the number of yearly deaths had been brought down from 30,000 to 4,000; the number of cases annually from "millions" to some 250,000.

Grants for Development

These grants are usually designated to finance projects from which no immediate return can be expected. Aid in this category might provide a village with a water supply; might build a hospital, a school, a bridge or a highway; it might train a group of teachers or finance a reforestation project. The aid may be made available in the form of money, materials, equipment, or even surplus food, especially where a participating country also contributes funds, labor, and materials.

Some critics of foreign aid are inclined to be skeptical as to whether such grants are really necessary. Why are such grants necessary? In many developing countries, people have not had the benefits of industrial revolution and social reform enjoyed by countries of the West. They are not only poor to begin with, but such capital as they have is in the hands of the few who use it for their own purposes. Under these conditions, reform comes slowly. If we in the U.S. wait for capital to be generated from within, famine and revolution are likely to come first.

The broad base for the sort of tax structure which makes steady improvement in our own public services possible is absent. Such taxable property as exists is in the hands of the minority. "Seed capital" for improvements which the people need right now must be provided, for the time being, from sources outside the country.

The citizens of some nations are already burdening themselves to pay for improvements. In most cases, they ask only the minimum amount of outside funds they need. Being "underdeveloped" they need much and they need it all at once, escaping only now from centuries of physical and social erosion. Grants, therefore, are a means of buying time while their own resources can be organized.

A program which began with a project to improve the lot of some farmers in Peru illustrates how a relatively small sum made available at the right time can produce results out of proportion to the size of the investment.

Some way was being sought to help the impoverished farmers of the altiplano to break out of their unending cycle of poverty and debt. These *campesinos,* unlike their North American counterparts, had no way to borrow money either from the bank or from the government at reasonable rates of interest.

The only solution open to them and to millions in the same predicament was to help themselves. And the only way they could generate their own capital was through the formation of a cooperative credit society.

Parenthetically, the very word "cooperative" is still frightening to many around the world who see in it overtones of socialism and even Communism. But in actual fact, the cooperative, and the cooperative credit society in particular, offer the impoverished farmer his only chance to become a capitalist, on however small a scale.

Wherever cooperative societies are to be introduced, the first requirement—even before "seed capital"—is a trained and expert leadership. With this in mind, in 1963, AID allocated $160,000 for the training of such leaders, not only for the farmers of the altiplano but for other countries of Latin America.

By 1964, the Credit Union National Association of Madison, Wisconsin, through this grant, had set up a center for the training of these leaders in Lima, Peru, with an initial enrollment of more than forty. When these graduates scatter out over the continent, to be followed by others in successive years, an incalculable stimulus could result, not only to cooperatives, but indeed to the principle of self-help and self-reliance throughout the continent.

Not all development grants turn out so well, as witness one approved to build a highway in Pakistan between Karachi and Quetta, 600 miles to the north. It was believed that this highway would speed the economic progress of the nation and would also considerably strengthen the military bastion of the region.

Following a survey, substantial amounts of money and materials in the form of cement, graders, trucks, and even food, were allocated over a period of years. AID also provided engineers under technical assistance.

But as it turned out, the cost of constructing the highway over primitive and unknown terrain had been underestimated. Stubborn rock formations causing frequent breakdown of equipment presented problems that had not been anticipated. As a last straw, Pakistan, short of funds and afflicted with political instability, withdrew its share of support. Today, construction is at a standstill even though the highway is badly needed.

Aid by Contract

Aid administered through contracts with other agencies represents an important development since the "turnaround year" of 1962. Although for some time projects have been carried out in this manner, they have increased sharply both in number and in variety.

Contracts may be arranged with colleges, universities, business firms, or private agencies. Their objectives may be: improvements in education, construction, agriculture, literacy and health programs, the distribution of surplus foods, and college teaching.

As of March, 1964, AID had 995 signed contracts in force

for projects in 70 countries. Of these, 252 were with colleges and universities; 187 with business firms; 120 with voluntary agencies. The others covered a wide range of organizations. In general, five types of agencies are eligible for contracts: colleges and universities; commercial firms; research associations; voluntary agencies; and foundations. The contracts called for an expenditure of approximately $400 million. In duration, they extended anywhere from a few weeks to several years.

Typical Projects Under Contract

Measured by the gradual growth of colleges in the West, the pace at which educational institutions in some of the underdeveloped countries are expanding is breath-taking. The University of Nigeria, for example, after only four years of existence, has colleges of the arts, social studies, science, and technology.

This growth has been made possible by an AID contract under which two institutions as distant in geography and culture as the University of Nigeria and Michigan State University are linked together.

On the University of Nigeria's faculty, nineteen nations are represented. Ninety-four are natives of the country; 59 are from the United States, and 14 from far-off India. The student body has grown from 200 in 1961 to 1,800 in 1964. One wonders what U.S. college could keep functioning with a 900 per cent increase in enrollment over three years!

In the industrial field, a U.S. firm has contracted through AID to rehabilitate a hydroelectric plant in South Korea, and has agreed to repair buildings and waterways, install new equipment, and train local applicants for the work of operation and maintenance.

A consultant firm has been engaged to advise businessmen in West Pakistan on the establishment of such small businesses as the manufacture of farm implements, roofing materials, electrical supplies, poultry appliances, and building hardware.

The Farmers' Union, an agricultural organization, has

consummated a unique arrangement under which young agronomists from Latin America were enabled to gain practical farming experience here in the States. An initial grant of $50,000 was made available by AID with the express purpose of building "bridges of good will."

Sixty-seven young men between the ages of 18 and 30 were brought here from several Latin American countries. They lived with families in Iowa, Wisconsin, the Dakotas, and Montana; they worked in the fields, studied 4-H Clubs and cooperatives, and took short courses at agricultural colleges.

Loans for Development

Loans rather than grants are made in cases where a financial return on the investment can ultimately be expected. They are made to increase the productivity of land, to build needed factories, power stations, or dams. The period allowed for repayment varies from a few years to forty years; interest rates, from 1 per cent to 5.5 per cent per annum.

Typical is a $5.5 million loan to the National Steel Company of Brazil, half owned by the government and half by stockholders. The loan enabled smelters and steel plants to expand production by 200,000 tons of ingots per year.

Food for Peace

About thirty miles up the Hudson River from New York City, a ghost fleet was riding at anchor a few years ago. On the autumn morning when I went there, the ships were a depressing sight—gray, silent, motionless.

I had made the trip because I knew that the ships were being used as improvised storage space. Side-by-side, their holds were packed with grain—the grain we could not eat and could not sell. To me, they epitomized many of the grain elevators and the familiar storage bins we may see filled to overflowing at many railroad stops across the Middle West.

The sight was not only saddening but embarrassing. I had

just come back from Guatemala with the words of an earnest public health worker still ringing in my ears: "The big problem for our Indian farmers is how to exist from one harvest to the next. In my district alone, there are 20,000 Indians who often survive for two or three months out of the year by gnawing roots."

A whistle blew. An ocean-going freighter hove to alongside one of the ghost ships. A winch began to whir. "Food for Peace," said the man beside me. "Our surplus is moving out. As a matter of fact, at any given moment there are at least thirty U.S. ships on the oceans of the world engaged in this mission to the hungry."

My conscience felt somewhat eased. Only a few of us appear to be familiar with the workings of that most important phase of foreign aid—the effort to share our abundance of food with the world's hungry.

Food for Peace is administered by U.S. AID, although the cost does not figure in the agency's budget. The U.S. Government pays for the food, which is not included in foreign aid appropriations. Contributions of food to a country then are in addition to foreign aid allocations. Food for Peace is in itself a sizable aid operation with food valued at $4 billion being distributed in 1965 alone.

The Food for Peace program serves a threefold purpose. It takes an embarrassing surplus off our hands which, if dumped on the home market, could bankrupt many U.S. farmers. It saves millions living at the ragged edge of existence from starvation. At the same time, it provides capital for development projects in ways which we shall presently consider.

Rarely has it happened that one of our laws is ever known by its number beyond our own shores. But Public Law 480—the law enacted by the Eighty-third Congress under which Food for Peace is distributed—has become a familiar word in 110 countries.

The surplus has come about through amazing progress made by the U.S. farmer in his ability to grow food. Public

Law 480 represents our government's ultimate success after years of trial and error in finding a way to keep ahead of the farmer's productivity.

The pivotal point in this situation came with the 1930's. It took the economic disaster of the depression to call attention to a fundamental fact of life—namely, that the farmer cannot turn off the cow, nor tell the Leghorn not to lay; nor can he command the crops to stop growing in the field.

When commodity prices hit rock bottom—eggs down from $.80 a dozen to $.12; wheat from $2.08 to $.40; beef cattle from $35 a hundredweight to $7—the government stepped in and began buying to hold produce off the market, in a desperate effort to avert disaster.

For the first time, to the man who raised it, surplus food was a curse. Then came World War II and its aftermath. Once more our attitude underwent a complete change. Food needed to nourish those left homeless by the war was no longer a blight. It was a blessing.

Since that time, although government price support has stirred continuous controversy, our attitude toward surplus food has never changed. We want to see it find its way to empty stomachs.

Except for the single hiatus of the depression period, the productivity of the U.S. farmer has moved forward rapidly over the years. In the time of Isaac Newton, our first Commissioner of Agriculture, appointed by President Lincoln in 1862, a farmer toiling from sunup to sundown produced barely enough food for himself and three others. But our efficiency grew. By 1900, a farmer was producing for himself and four others; by 1951, the ratio had jumped to himself and fourteen others.

Then, in the 1950's, came the most amazing strides of all. At the time of this writing (1965) the "average" farmer is producing enough for himself and thirty others.

In the years following World War II, small amounts of our wheat, beans, rice, corn, and powdered milk were sent abroad, mostly as relief. But our efforts to find world markets for our excess agricultural products were not notably successful. The reason was clear: the countries most in want were least able to pay in dollars. To cut prices and "dump" our surpluses abroad would have been injurious to the economies of other nations. Some way, then, had to be found for distributing our surplus without upsetting the delicate trade balance.

Public Law 480 comprises four main provisions called titles:

Title I. Most developing countries today find themselves short of dollar exchange. As one means of circumventing this handicap, under Title I, a country can pay for its food by depositing its own currency in one of its banks as credit to the account of the U.S. Our government can then make use of such funds for manifold purposes within that country's borders. Title I uses account for 60 per cent of the total surplus food program.

Title II. Famine, flood, or other disasters may strike anywhere at any time, causing death, destruction, and disease. In such situations, when large-scale reconstruction work is needed, Title II, often referred to as "food for work," is invoked. Under its provisions, men may be employed on such projects as dam-building, reforestation, or soil conservation, and receive part of their pay in food from the U.S. farmer's surplus.

Title III. Most of us are familiar with the humanitarian services of such voluntary organizations as the Red Cross, Church World Service, Catholic Relief Service, American Friends Service Committee, United Jewish Relief, CARE, and some agencies of the U.N. Through agreements with AID's Food for Peace program, these organizations make large amounts of food available as direct relief. About one-fourth of all the products allocated under Public Law 480 is distributed under the provisions of Title III. More than 72 million persons in 112 countries were recipients of relief in this form in 1963.

Title IV. Countries who wish to purchase outright wheat,

cotton, soybeans, butter, or other products, and pay for them in dollars through special credit arrangements, are able to do so under the provisions of Title IV.

Here are just a few representative accomplishments made possible by Public Law 480.

From Malarial Swamp to University

I first saw what could be achieved through funds of Title I in North India. The country had long been in dire need of rural universities. Training in agriculture, home economics, rural education, engineering, and the veterinary sciences, was available only in separate colleges, most of which were situated in cities. Facilities were inadequate. Leaders were of the opinion that a university situated in rural surroundings would prove a much more effective place in which to train the outstanding men and women that the nation so urgently needed. Furthermore, they reasoned, it should be possible to operate such a university at a lower cost in the country than in the city. For this purpose, the U.S. released a portion of the funds which India had put on deposit to purchase food under Title I.

Up near the foothills of the Himalayas was a large tract of almost abandoned land. Local residents had fled the area in large numbers because both the soil was so poor and the region was infested with malarial mosquitoes. Such a remote spot seemed an unpromising location for a large university. But the land was available, and it was cheap. Ground was broken in 1959.

In late 1961, I went to visit this new venture. The manager of the university farm met me at the railway station. "Don't expect too much," he said, as we drove the twelve miles out to the site of the new institution. "They've only been at it here for two years. First they had to wipe out malaria; then they had to fill gullies and bulldoze the hillocks to get the building program under way. Even now we're still putting our roots down.

"We began developing the farm first," he went on, "for the farm must help support the university. Students will work here to earn part of their keep. I tell you, it's an exciting thing to watch a university grow—from the swamps up like this."

We stopped near a group of modern buildings. They were made from brick fired on the spot. The administration hall was almost finished. Other buildings were in various stages of completion. Laborers, carpenters, and masons were gathering, getting ready to begin the day's work. Over at one side an American consultant from the University of Illinois was poring over a blueprint with the Indian engineers.

Later that evening, as we drove back to the railway station, I thought of my old neighbors in Ohio, of how proud they would be—of how proud any U.S. farmer would be—to see what purpose had been served by the surplus production of his acres over here, halfway across the world. My neighbors would have been reassured to learn that India herself was paying more than half the cost, which made our contribution under Public Law 480 all the more meaningful.

Two weeks later I was in West Pakistan. A supervisor of education named Hajat Khan wanted particularly to show me a school in his village. It was one of sixteen hundred which had been built in the country during the past three years. Sheet metal for the roofs, cement for the walls, and hardware for the interiors had all been bought by Title I funds, released for that purpose. The village people had volunteered their labor.

"We're putting up schools as fast as our funds permit," said Hajat Khan. "But it's hardly fast enough. If it weren't for the extra schools made possible by Public Law 480, 185,000 children would be growing up in Pakistan today deprived of the chance for any schooling at all."

Men and Trees

A striking example of the use of Food for Peace funds to promote a worthy purpose took place in Algeria. Here the job was done under Title II.

Revolution and independence, followed by the departure of many French citizens who held key positions, left millions with nothing to do, many at the point of starvation. A down-to-earth program was needed—one which would provide work for many hands and at the same time give the Algerians something in which they could participate with enthusiasm. The new government couldn't undertake such a job. It had its hands full keeping down revolts.

The answer was finally found in a program for reclaiming thousands of acres of desert by planting 21 million forest seedlings on them. Merely to dig so many holes and to keep the seedlings watered and cared for until they can take root is in itself a monumental undertaking in terms of man hours. Today the program employs more than 20,000 workmen. Church World Service and other voluntary agencies are lending technical personnel and assisting with the distribution of food.

This could not have been possible without the availability of food under Title II, for the laborers received a substantial part of their pay in wheat flour, soybeans, and powdered milk under that provision of the law. This is "food work" in its most literal interpretation. But more than that, it is a beacon lighting the way to a brighter future.

City of the Hopeful

The world-wide school lunch program is also under Public Law 480. I had heard much about it, and I was curious to see it at work.

It was almost noon when I reached a slum settlement on the outskirts of Lima. Here, I was told, was a new kind of slum. I could clearly see the fresh encrustation of new, flimsy shelters reaching up the steep hillside, an expression of rising hope.

All large Latin American cities have appalling slums on their perimeters. But this was different—this sudden springing up of what are known as *barriadas*—communities of the hopeful. They are a phenomenon of today.

This particular *barriada* was made up of about seventy families. They had all come from the same village, about 165 miles from Lima. It was the familiar story. Driven to desperation by the condition of their lives—no land, no work, and no food—they had decided to make a break and try their luck elsewhere. They had rented two battered trucks, crammed in the women, children, grandparents, and made the trip to Lima in two days. Arriving in the middle of the night, they had settled on the open space on which several younger men had staked a claim some weeks before. This was a barren plot that no one could possibly want, above other slums on the rocky hillside.

The migration had taken place two or three months ago. But already this "city of the hopeful" was beginning to show signs of permanence. The inhabitants had made walls for their houses out of bamboo mats. They had roofed them over with sheets of tin from oil drums. Here and there were mounds of earth and raw holes in the hillside. Some had dug caves for their families where they would manage to exist until things took an upward turn. Others already had acquired several sheets of corrugated metal which they used as shelter from the elements.

The lull of midday lay over the hillside. In the distance, someone banged away, shoring up his new home. One enterprising young fellow, having rescued an old tire from a refuse heap, was busy carving it up into pieces which he would then fashion into sandals and sell. Most of the men and many of the women were away in the city, looking for work—any kind of work.

"But where are the children?" I asked my guide.

"Oh, they're all at the school, about half a mile down the hill."

I said I would like to see them, and off we went. We got there just at lunch time. Outside the low, rambling building the youngsters stood waiting in rows of four. They were ragged, but they were clean. They smiled happily as they chattered among themselves.

Suddenly a hush fell. They bowed their heads to give

thanks for their food. Then they began moving. They paused before two large pots where four women volunteers were standing ready with ladles and spoons. Some children carried plates, some carried bowls; some had only classroom slates on which to receive food.

An intriguing aroma came from the two pots. The meal consisted of wheat bulgur, which is wheat that has first been cracked, then steamed and dried for shipment abroad. When cooked, it fluffs up like rice. Mixed with beans and other vegetables and flavored with spices, wheat bulgur is nourishing and delicious.

The next day I visited Richard Apodoca, our AID officer in Peru, to learn more about the school lunch program under which these children had received their noon meal.

"Here's how it operates," he said. "The U.S. brings the food as far as the port of entry. There the Peruvian Government and some private agencies take over and carry it by train and truck to wherever it is needed.

"Distribution to the children is handled on the spot by parent-teacher associations. There are now 980 of them in Peru, set up for just this purpose. The associations themselves provide nutritional supplements, such as meat, fish, spices, vegetables, and fruit. The cooking and serving is done by women volunteers."

"What sort of a job is the program doing?" I asked.

"I'll say this," Apodoca replied. "According to the Ministry of Education, more than 300,000 Peruvian school children are receiving a warm meal a day because of it.

"But statistics don't tell the story," he went on. "You've no idea what that meal means to these youngsters. Remember, a lot of them walk to school, some a distance of anywhere from two to four miles. If it weren't for that hot lunch, they'd be too weak to get much out of their studies. Ministry of Education records show that in schools where they serve the lunch, enrollment has increased by as much as 35 per cent. What's more, if it weren't for that food, a lot of parents would have to let their children go to work."

"But isn't this going to make them too dependent on the school?"

"Quite the contrary. Many are learning for the first time the relationship of nutrition to health."

Later I learned that altogether 32 million children in 80 countries were benefiting, like the children in Lima, from the school lunch program.

One would have to be blindly unrealistic to assume that all the food which goes abroad under Public Law 480 is put to such worthy uses as have been described. Some of it undoubtedly finds its way to those who are quite capable of looking after themselves. Some of it turns up on the black market where it is often sold at exorbitant prices to those poor souls for whom it was intended to be given.

But foreign aid officers are generally aware of such loopholes as exist and are doing much to plug them. In short, if we do not lose heart and have the vision and detachment to profit by our experience, it should be possible for us steadily to improve this worthy program.

Food for Peace has a human appeal not inherent in other technical forms of aid such as technical assistance or development grants and loans. But it would be quite wrong to fall into the comfortable assumption that our surplus production in itself could ever offer anything like an adequate solution to the world's hunger.

Although our food shipments are of immeasurable help, it is easy to see how pitiably small is such aid when compared with the world food deficit. In 1964, our total Food for Peace shipments could have alleviated no more than 5 per cent of the world's food shortage for that year. Indeed, if the entire American food surplus in a given year were shipped abroad at one time, it would stop hunger for only about three weeks.

We must do all that we reasonably can do, but in the long run there is only one valid answer: That is to grow as much food as possible at the places where it is needed.

4

A LOOK AT ACHIEVEMENTS

FOREIGN AID is an elephant," observed the author of an article in the November 5, 1963, issue of *The Christian Century*. The analogy is not concerned with the agency's size but with the adage of the blind man who tries to "see" the elephant.

Many of us, notes the author, are in the same position. Until the blind man had explored the ears, the tusks, the vast flanks and felt the rough-grained hide, he could have no conception of the beast. Nor can we with foreign aid, until we have gained at least some acquaintance with its operations.

Even then, evaluation is difficult. The most self-assured expert would hesitate to make a categorical judgment on its tangible accomplishments to date. Foreign aid can't be weighed on a scale, measured with a yardstick, or charted on a graph showing that 1964 was bigger or better than the year before. It is therefore easier for some to shrug the whole thing off with a ringing phrase such as "money down the drain."

Even among those on the scene, opinion is often divided. This was brought home to me on a recent trip through Latin America. I was speaking with an AID program analyst in one of the smaller countries. He was dispirited.

"We aren't getting anywhere," he said. "We've been here for ten years and what have we got to show for it? Do you know even the per acre yield of corn, after all this time, is actually going down?"

On the other hand, a veteran agriculturist attached to the AID mission in the same country, talked to me that afternoon in a different key.

"When we first came here," he said, "only the well-to-do—no more than a handful of families—could afford pasteurized milk. It was not only expensive, but you almost needed a doctor's prescription to buy it. What's more, its purity was doubtful. All that's changed now. Modern dairies are springing up in cities and small towns where farmers can send their milk to be pasteurized and then sold in sealed bottles. This advance brings pure milk within reach of thousands who were denied it before; it also means more income for the farmers."

"How much credit should be given to AID for all this?"

He shrugged. "That's hard to say. But this much is sure. We were here, we talked it up, we spread the word. We got people interested in better herds and modern equipment, then loaned them the money to make a start. And by the way, you should see the new flocks of imported Leghorns. They really thrive here."

I was puzzled. Conflicting viewpoints could hardly be true. Yet the more I thought, the more it became clear that this was possible. The decline in corn yields could be accounted for by the fact that as the population increased, more and more farmers were pushed farther up the mountainside onto eroded land, where the low yields from their infertile acres brought down the national average.

The success of the milk and poultry projects, on the other hand, was no doubt due in large part to the ample supply of low cost, improved feeds made available from the U.S.

Perhaps another reason for the marked lack of enthusiasm on the part of the general public is that foreign aid achievements in this thrill-hungry world are not of the sort that can compete for headlines.

Several years ago in upper New York State, a small boy fell into an abandoned well. The details of his rescue were flashed to the public hour after hour by radio and the wire services until he was brought to safety. Black headlines proclaimed his rescue; the nation rejoiced.

At about the same time, locusts appeared in black clouds, darkening the skies over Iran, Ethiopia, Syria, Arabia, Pakistan, and North India. It was a danger that had threatened these regions recurringly since the days of the Pharaohs, when, according to Exodus X:4–5 we find that locusts "covered the face of the whole earth so that the land was darkened . . . and there remained not any green thing."

When the locusts hove in sight in that particular year, the wheat on which millions depended for survival was already in the head, which made the situation unusually desperate.

Promptly FAO, the Food and Agricultural Organization of the U.N., went into action. But FAO operating on its own was not equipped to launch an all-out attack over so large an area. Point Four officials got word of the gathering locust blight. They telephoned and volunteered their services. Governments of ten other countries followed suit.

Veteran pest fighters equipped with low-flying duster planes and quantities of powerful insecticide were dispatched to the scene within a matter of hours. Like the famous tank war in North Africa, the struggle surged back and forth over many miles. But in the end, millions of tons of grain were saved. Widespread famine was averted. The lives of thousands were saved by this carefully planned and scientifically executed operation.

The campaign was exciting to those who took part in it. The press, however, gave it only the slightest mention, nothing like the prominence accorded the rescue of the little toddler from the well. The drama of the war against the locusts was dissipated by distance, the numbers involved, and the time span over which it took place.

The same holds true for most foreign aid undertakings. It is even more difficult for the average person to form a clear concept of its operation, because the agency so often functions, as in the case of the locust war, in collaboration with other agencies, or with workers in the host countries. In our reports, we should give due credit to other agencies.

The very words commonly employed to describe the participating nations—"underdeveloped" or "developing"—are in themselves misleading. These words conjure up a picture of nations blessed with rich virgin soil and abundant resources only awaiting the magic wand of technology to unlock their treasures.

But these countries, their soil worn out, their once luxuriant forests gone, lacking capital, lacking technology, must turn to the more favored countries for their salvation. It is here one can make a case that our foreign aid program has already justified itself. By giving "a leg up" at a time when it was critically needed, foreign aid has implemented the first difficult steps along the road to freedom for several countries.

Engineering and Industry

In some developing countries—water, simply water—which we in the West so often take for granted—tops the list of crucial needs. Often scarce, it is of the first importance, for land that is irrigated can produce, year in, year out, about 30 per cent more than land that is not irrigated.

India, with its great arid stretches, is a country with a special need for water. Some things I saw during my first years there indelibly impressed on my mind the significance of scarce water.

As I traveled over Northwest India, the territory of Kipling's Kim, where the plains fan out from the base of the Himalaya Mountains, I saw the farmers laboriously watering small fields by hand, a bucketful at a time. Farther on, two men, with the help of a yoke of oxen, were lifting a larger amount from a well, using a big leather bag.

My Indian agriculturist companion told me that two men, working without respite all day, could barely lift enough water to irrigate one acre. But the same acre would have to be watered every five days.

He shaded his eyes with his hands and looked northward where the Himalayas loomed blue and hazy in the far distance. "There," he said, "is one of nature's great ironies. Up there, where nobody needs it, the rain falls in torrents. The plain here, on the other hand, has the lowest mean average rainfall of any place in the country. Once a year the great Sutlej River hustles all the rainfall to the sea where nobody needs it. In between, everybody needs it. And nobody gets it. Ah, well—someday."

Ever since the beginning of India's First Five-Year Plan, the building of dams for irrigation and power was given high priority. By far the most ambitious power project on the drawing boards was the building of the great Bhakra Dam and the harnessing of the Sutlej. It was also the most significant, because it could result in the irrigation of 3.5 million acres of cropland.

It would be unfair to imply that no one had ever thought of bringing the unruly Sutlej under control before India became independent. For more than fifty years, both Indian and British engineers had watched the gray waters roll unchecked over the countryside during the monsoon, then subside in the dry season to such a trickle that the women had to wade out to the center of it to get enough water to do their washing.

But both the physical and the psychological obstacles were formidable. Among the physical: The first monsoon would sweep away with its awful force any foundations laid during the previous dry season. The project would take at least five years, and the river would have to be diverted into temporary channels during that time.

As for the psychological: The farmers who would benefit most weren't for it, since it would mean surrendering a part of their holdings which had come down to them from their ancestors, in order to create canals and ditches. "What good is irrigation," they argued, "if it takes away our land?"

Many of India's future engineers were studying at colleges abroad when Mr. Nehru, in one of his first speeches as Prime Minister made his memorable statement: "There is no time to walk. We must take off on the run."

The young men, on fire with patriotic fervor, took these words as a personal challenge: The Sutlej must be dammed. For India, the question no longer was *can* it be done, but *how soon?* Engineers were assigned to draw up blueprints. Experts, among them G. I. Savage and Harvey Slocum of Boulder Dam fame, were called in for consultation from other countries.

Work began in 1950, a step at a time. But the country lacked the funds to finance such an enormous enterprise. Statesman Morarji Desai, adamant in his insistence that the money must be found, dramatized his point with the ringing declaration: "We must tax ourselves down to our bread today if we would have the means for a better tomorrow."

As engineers worked out the construction details, they found the projected feat overwhelming. To mention just one headache, two huge tunnels, each fifty feet in diameter would have to be blasted through solid rock for a distance of one-half mile to divert the Sutlej into its temporary channels.

When I paid my first visit to the construction site of Bhakra Dam in 1952, I wished that some of those who still imagined India only as a place where underfed millions sat indolently, staring impassively at sacred cows, could have been with me.

Here was a new India of the twentieth century where the muscle of excess hands was being skillfully blended with the power of the most specialized machines. What must yesterday have been a scene of pastoral calm was now a forest of derricks, cranes, draglines, scoops, and bulldozers.

From the bottom of the trench to the top of the embankment three hundred feet above, a continuous chain of men in mudstained dhotis and women in their varicolored saris, all standing less than a foot apart, passed heavy basins of earth to one another in the cadence of a rhythmical chant. More than 100,000 were at work that day, many newly trained on jobs they never knew existed a few weeks ago.

From close by came the deafening rat-tat-tat of a jack-hammer. Turning, I saw a lithe young Indian, wearing only shorts and a mask to protect his eyes from flying chips. He held the clattering machine to its course with the assurance of a veteran, cutting the huge rock to precise measurement.

His name, he said, was Naran Singh, and he came from a village a few miles away. Up until six weeks ago, when he had gone into training, he had never done anything but farm. He liked this job better; it paid better, and he hoped he could find another job now that he knew how to do it, when this one was finished. Of Naran Singh and men like him the new India will be made up.

In a small, hot, board shack, an Indian engineer pointed to the blueprints on his drafting table and said: "Next to your Boulder Dam, our waterhead, at 740 feet, will be the highest in the world. The lead-off canal will be 400 feet wide, and deep enough to float one of your largest steamships. There'll be a network of branch canals—3,000 of them in all—carrying water to nearly 4 million acres."

When I came back to that area in 1963, I would not have recognized the place. From the air, instead of the predominant barren brown, with only patches of green here and there, we saw a solid carpet of green broken only by the glint of sunlight on the crisscross of canals. It was the green of cotton crops, and citrus orchards, of hybrid corn, yes, and of potatoes, for it had been found that the tuber could be adapted to India.

But as we traveled around for a closer look at things, the most gratifying change we saw was in the faces and attitudes of the farmers themselves. Their former look of hopelessness had been replaced with an air of confidence that with the help of water they were going to win for a change, and would keep on winning.

The Bhakra Dam, although the largest, is only one of twenty-seven major river developments for irrigation and cheap electric power which India has brought to completion in the years since 1952. Of these, AID has participated in twelve through grants, loans, and the services of engineers. Although our help in making these projects possible was significant, we paid only a fraction of the cost. In all cases, the Indian Government contributed at least 80 per cent of the funds.

Our foreign aid program has played its part in making possible the development of other great rivers around the world. Among them are the Volta River project in Ghana, the Mekong in Southeast Asia, others in Nigeria, Nicaragua, Iran, Korea, and the Philippines.

All of these are enduring achievements which can bring not only food, but hope for the future, to millions. (The Bhakra Dam alone is supplying water today to 1.18 million farm families.)

Aid in Ethiopia

The examples cited above pertain to single projects, but far more common in all countries is the integrated program of one-half dozen or more projects.

Let us take the case of Ethiopia. The world outside has turned upside down several times since Emperor Hailé Selassie ascended the throne. Yet, in 1964, while the rest of the continent emerged from the past in many instances with violent and shattering change, the Lion of Judah led his people slowly and quietly.

The country's strategic location in northeastern Africa abutting the Gulf of Aden gives it an importance beyond its wealth or the size of its population. A weakened Ethiopia could easily fall victim to an aggressor as it has in the past; a strong Ethiopia could become a beacon lighting the way for all of Africa to enduring political and economic freedom.

The nation occupies an area almost twice the size of Texas, comprising 400,000 square miles, with a population of some 17 million. Geographically it is distinguished by its wide differences in altitude, ranging from miasmic jungles at 450 feet below sea level to great, grassy plateaus at 7,000 feet. It has great resources in its soil, its forests, and its minerals, and abundant water for power. Yet all these resources remain largely undeveloped.

AID's first Director saw Ethiopia as an area crucial to the world's destiny. Ever since that time, it has been an object of thoughtful planning. Funds have been allocated over six basic sectors, according to the following percentages: agriculture, 32; education, 15; public health and sanitation, 12; Blue Nile River Valley development, 10; industry and roads, 8; miscellaneous, 23.

Agricultural development has been advanced through education, the experiment station, and the extension service. With the help of AID, two centers have been set up for the training of agricultural workers. One is the College of Agriculture and Mechanical Arts which has graduated 140 young men, trained to play key roles in the program. The other is the Agricultural-Technical School which is developing younger workers as field demonstrators.

An Ethiopian heads the experiment station where new varieties of crops and livestock are introduced and tested. Studies are also conducted here on such daily problems as the suitability of farm implements, methods of applying fertilizer, and improved facilities for grain storage.

Ethiopia is a country thirsting for education, yet lacking in almost everything. Schools must be built, teachers trained, courses of study outlined, even textbooks must be written. AID is helping to get some of these things done. The Emperor and the Ministry of Education have expressed their feeling about the importance of the work in these words: "Education opens the way to material and spiritual life and is the strongest instrument for the preservation of the country and its liberties."

One of Ethiopia's economic problems is unique, arising

from a custom of the country. The people, whether city or country dwellers, swathe themselves in great lengths of cotton cloth as a sort of national costume. The nation, therefore, was spending more than $1 million annually on importing cotton cloth, although heavy machinery, chemicals, hardware, and other critical imports were urgently needed.

Local weavers, working on their crude hand looms were able to produce only strips some six inches wide which then had to be stitched together into clothing.

A privately owned weaving mill was modernized and expanded with a development loan of $500,000. It now supplies a major share of the needed cotton cloth, reducing the import drain proportionately.

Among other projects claiming one-fifth of the foreign aid funds are experimental housing and staff for public administration.

Meeting the Leadership Emergency

In the early days of Point Four, wherever American specialists went abroad they ran against the same obstacle that had baffled their opposite numbers in the participating countries for years: How to communicate technical information in a minimum length of time to millions of farmers who were not only rooted in traditional ways of doing things, but who were also largely illiterate.

Technicians were needed immediately by the hundreds to go into the villages and teach the farmers. In India alone the First Five-Year Plan called for 60,000 of these workers. They were to be called *gram sevaks,* servants to the villagers.

But nowhere were there enough men already trained for this job. The first step then was to find the men to teach those who in turn were to teach the farmers. There were far from enough men available in the host countries to take on this work. The few who were qualified already had their hands full coping with other problems in their emerging countries. Nor were there anywhere the necessary facilities —classrooms, equipment, and so on—for such a training program.

Apparently a number of Point Four workers in the field all got the same message back to Washington at the same time: "Teachers must be found to teach the village servants, and sent to the United States for training."

Washington reacted quickly and favorably. The U.S. Department of Agriculture, with its long experience in such endeavors, made its facilities available. In 1950, the first year of foreign aid, 1,710 trainees arrived on our shores. They came from 22 different countries. Some could be spared from their jobs back home for only a few weeks. Others were to remain for anywhere from three months to a year.

USDA took responsibility for their accommodation and their training, started them off with an orientation course in Washington, then dispersed them around the country on previously arranged assignments to agricultural colleges, county extension agents, cooperatives, dairies, and food processing plants. At one time or another, many were guests in farm homes; some worked on farms.

Most of the ideas picked up by these alert young men and women will probably never be known and certainly could not be listed here. But these are just two of them:

Justina Anazonn from Nigeria, while studying home economics at Ohio University, put an oven together of discarded kerosene tins and sheets of asbestos which could be inexpensively duplicated by West African homemakers who cannot afford the models offered for sale in stores.

A chemist from Colombia, a student at Purdue, worked out means whereby potatoes could be stored without rotting for up to eight months. His development has great importance for Latin America where as much as one-half the potato crop may be lost each year through rotting.

It was not only the visitors who gained from the experience.

An Ohio farmer said: "The countries may be underdeveloped, but the people certainly aren't. My two guests kept me on my toes all the time. They wanted yes and no answers —and no fooling."

A county extension agent told me: "It was a broadening experience. Their problems are different, tougher than ours. But we're both essentially after the same things."

Said a professor in an agricultural college: "When I think of the responsible positions these men and women will hold some day, I am grateful that we can have some little part in their training."

By 1951, the number of trainees—now coming from Asia, the Near East, Africa, and Latin America—had jumped to 3,625. More have come each year, with the peak annual influx of 6,779 in 1960. This part of the foreign aid program was successful from the beginning and continued to remain so.

Here was a chain reaction at work. By 1964, 70,000 promising young people as well as mature workers from other lands had received training and experience of this sort in the U.S. They had been exposed to the real, working America, not the America of Hollywood so often portrayed by films sent abroad.

They had returned home, each to a technical job or to train hundreds of village servants who in turn would instruct thousands of farmers. The experience, the impressions, of a single man or woman would therefore re-echo a hundredfold. None of this can be weighed or put on a flow chart. But it exists.

Emphasis is now being placed on the training of technical workers in their own countries, in the midst of their own problems and situations. Ideally, that is where the training should be done.

4-H Goes Abroad

Will Rogers once said: "With all the hoop-la ideas we Americans have, every once in a while we hit a good one; 4-H club is such an idea."

The 4-H signifies the four foundation stones of the program: development of the heart, hands, head, and health. Under the motto "to make the best better" club members produce better seed, grow gardens, raise prize livestock, sew, preserve foods, care for the sick, and develop other projects that are of help to people.

It was natural that the spread of the 4-H program to other lands should be a prime objective of Point Four from the very first. 4-H didn't need a great amount of funds—much could be done with seed, a few simple tools, and local resources.

Progress was slow in the beginning, due to a shortage of well-equipped leaders. Also, in most developing countries young people are not expected to have farm or home projects of their own or make decisions. But it has picked up momentum as the years have gone by. Today, 4-H Clubs with adaptations have been formed in fifteen countries in Latin America; three in Africa; four in the Near East; and six in Asia. Every boy and girl trained in improved ways of doing things today will exert an influence on the way the people of his country live tomorrow.

Soon after the New Year, in 1964, I stopped in Guatemala to meet Alfredo Enriques, 4-H Club AID Adviser for that country. My visit was well-timed. The rural youth clubs happened to be holding their annual meeting at the National Agricultural School. We left at once for the school, about twenty miles from Guatemala City.

Enriques is about forty-five; he was a hard-working county agent in New Mexico for many years before he joined the AID staff. We entered the school auditorium where 360 club members were holding their public speaking contest. The brilliantly lighted rostrum was decorated with national flags. The twenty-two contestants stood at attention on the rostrum until their names were called. It was an impressive and inspiring sight.

Presiding in this august chamber was a chunky lad of about eleven, in T shirt and overalls. All the boys in the contest were similarly dressed; the girls wore either club uniforms or blue frocks that they had made themselves.

In a clear, full voice our young master of ceremonies, Victor Costello, announced the names of each of the twenty-two contestants. Their subject was: "What 4-S Means to Me." Some of the speakers were tall, some short. For each, Victor carefully adjusted the microphone. The five judges were exacting, disqualifying any contestant whose grammar was faulty, or who spoke from notes.

During an intermission, I was introduced to Mariano Palacio, district supervisor of agricultural extension and rural youth work.

"What do the 4-S's mean?" I asked.

"They represent the 4-H's rendered into Spanish," he said. "*Servir* is for service—the hand; *sentir* is for spirit—the heart; *salud* is for health—the body; *saber* is for knowledge and skill—the head."

When the contest was over, three winners were announced: The first prize, a brass trophy, went to ten-year-old Martha Hernandes. The second and third medals were won by boys.

"I see you're strict about handing out awards here."

"Yes," replied Alfredo, "much more so, I think, than in the States. I sometimes think that we don't keep our standards high enough at home. If the prizes are too big, or too easy to win, they can spoil the purpose of club work. Actually, we refused grants of prize money from several business firms this year. We want first of all to develop young people for rural leadership."

In the exhibit hall, proud young people stood beside the products they had brought from their homes, the results of their patient endeavor. We saw superior grains, fruits, vegetables, improved chickens, homemade feeders for poultry and swine. In the homemaking division, we admired the fine stitching and the intricate designs of table-runners, aprons, blouses, and other articles of clothing, as well as the rows of glass jars displaying preserved fruits and vegetables.

"Have the 4-S members done all of this alone?" I wondered.

Palacio smiled. "I studied your 4-H Club work in the States." Then he chided: "There, too, you have overzealous parents, uncles, and aunts, who want to help their boys and girls to win. We have the same problem here. But we avoid that as much as we can."

The next day I saw a practical exhibition by the young people at work. The 360 delegates were gathered in 20 separate groups. In each group, they took turns showing and explaining how to do many things, from selecting a good laying hen, to baking a loaf of bread, or designing a dress. One lad of fourteen showed how to graft the twig of an improved orange tree to native stock. As he demonstrated the graft, he explained the reasons for each step in the clear, concise terms of a good teacher. Questions were shot at him rapidly by his audience. He handled them with ease.

Guatemala today has around 2,000 4-S Club members. One-third of them are girls. Among the boys, the favorite projects are raising sugar cane, hybrid corn, chickens, vegetable crops, and livestock. Among the girls: food canning, sewing, cooking, home decoration, gardening, music, and flower arranging.

Elsewhere in Latin America, there are about 110,000 club members. This figure may seem cause for self-congratulation until we are reminded that in this area there are 30 million young people between ten and twenty years of age. Only one out of some 130 is getting any club experience at all.

Among those young people of the land, one felt a sense of confidence, an enthusiasm for the future. I was reminded of something Benjamin Disraeli once said: "It is a holy sight to see a nation saved by its youth."

There are many disappointments due to the lack of leaders. Many clubs have failed because the 4-H organization was merely exported without being adapted to the native culture. Some foreign aid workers in their haste did not take the trouble to develop volunteer club leaders, who are the kingpins of the 4-H movement. But from what I saw in Guatemala and elsewhere it seems apparent that the development of rural youth clubs has been well worth the effort.

Of course, 4-H has not pioneered everywhere. Young Farmers and Homemakers clubs, the British counterpart, was active long before 4-H in a number of African countries, chiefly Nigeria, Ghana, and the Rhodesias. Wherever I have met their members and leaders, I have been impressed by the quality of their work.

Better Crop Yields

When a U.S. farmer casts about for ways to increase his crop yields, he thinks first of seed and fertilizer. To get such high yields, our farmers have sought out new varieties of seeds and applied new chemical fertilizers in massive doses. It was natural, therefore, that early workers who went abroad thought first of fertilizers; not only had fertilizers worked wonders at home, but they seemed to be particularly needed in regions where the soil was weary and run-down after some four thousand years of cropping. The first serious effort was made in India; this country has also kept the most complete record of its achievements.

Even there, fieldmen found that the very farmers they were there to help would ask with some suspicion: "What *is* this 'plant food'? How do we know it won't ruin our land? What will it cost?"

In 1954, our aid program spent $3 million in India to finance fertilizer demonstrations. The attempt to distribute such huge amounts of fertilizer so quickly was bound to result in considerable waste.

In Gujarat State, several carloads of fertilizer, left out in the open through carelessness, were destroyed by the monsoon rains. In other locations, politicians got their hands on some shipments and dealt it out to win favor with the voters. Some of it was so improperly applied that it burned the crops. Those with an axe to grind made the most of these disappointments in an effort to discredit the early trials.

But the initial purpose—to stimulate interest in fertilizers—had been served. Indian technicians and farmers together pursued the experiments. Laboratories were set up for field research. At the time the program began, India was producing only 25,000 tons of fertilizer a year, and most of it—ammonium sulphate—was produced only as a by-product in the making of coke.

Since 1952, two developments have taken place: First, with U.S. technical counsel, the Fertilizer Association of India has been established as a responsible agency for research and the maintenance of standard grades. And second, Indian-operated fertilizer plants have been established, with a capacity of 347,000 tons per year. Plants to be completed by the close of 1965 are expected to bring the annual capacity up to 1 million tons.

"One-Man" Projects

Although, as noted earlier, most fieldmen work in collaboration with persons of other agencies, or of the host country, there are instances where an individual, because of some special flair, develops what has come to be called a "one-man" project. The term is not correct, however, for each one-man project depends on the contributions of many others whose names may never become associated with it.

One illustration is the work of Earl Brockman in Vietnam. His novel idea for increasing the food supply of embattled Vietnam has helped to raise living standards for thousands of farmers. "The formula is simple," he says. "Surplus corn, plus eight bags of cement for a homemade pigpen, plus three little pigs equals a better life for a family."

The program only got under way in 1962, but it has already put 5,000 families into the pig-raising business. AID hopes that by 1967, at least 100,000 families will be raising pigs. According to Brockman, the project works like this: "Our foreign aid program supplies the cement for the pigpens. A Vietnam cooperative agency distributes the corn. The pigs allotted to the program were produced by crossbreeding stock imported from America and Korea.

"This is not a giveaway," he says firmly. "The farmer, with borrowed money, buys a sow for breeding, and two little pigs which he will raise for sale. He also gets cement on credit to build his sty, and corn for feed from American surplus feed. The pig raisers pick up the corn at their local cooperative and trundle it home in pushcarts.

"Ever since I'd been in Vietnam, I'd been looking for a way to do something like that. Now pigs, corn, and cement are it.

"After we got started, we wore out a lot of shoe leather going from one village to another trouble shooting and trying to stop it before it got started. Some pigs got sick; some died on us. Some farmers got discouraged and quit. But by the end of the year, we were convinced we had something that would work for the country as a whole."

According to a recent survey, nine out of ten farmers on the pig project said it had raised the level of living for their families considerably. I have often wondered what conditions in Vietnam might be like today if, instead of one Earl Brockman, there had been one hundred like him, moving among the villagers, helping them, and making friends by means of the many simple projects they so badly need.

I learned of another successful one-man project in Iraq. Henry Botch was assigned in 1954, as an AID extension man in Kirkuk, to help the farmers in the northern part of the country modernize their methods. Botch, a graduate of Montana State College, was also to train twenty-six young Iraqis who had already graduated from the University of Ankara, to be extension agents.

He got into his jeep, went out and toured the country, and came back with a pretty good idea of what ought to be done. Then he went into the villages and began to hold forth on such topics as better ways of plowing, the need to plant a forage crop, and improved ways of fighting the insect plagues.

He did this for two months. Not a single farmer was willing to accept his advice. How could anyone trained in far-off America, and just arrived in their country, be able to tell them anything about how to do things? "The fathers of our fathers have been farming this way for centuries," the farmers said. "They must have known what they were doing."

One cold, rainy day in December, Henry Botch was

stranded in a remote village when the headman got to telling him about the scourge of rats they had just been having. As he showed Botch the havoc wreaked in their storage bins and on the new plant seedlings out in the fields, he shook his head sadly and said: "The poor Iraqi farmer! He gives one-third of his crop to the landlord, and one-third to the man who gives him his seed. The last third he shares with the rats."

It was all Henry needed to hear. That night he declared war on rats. He enlisted farmers of the village and sent for all the chemicals he could lay hands on. In due time he and the farmers had freed that village from rats. In view of the villagers' past experience, this was nothing short of a miracle. His fame spread. He became the Iraqis' Pied Piper. Hundreds of requests for his services began pouring in from other villages. Henry and his crew fanned out. In one and one-half months of diligent work, they got programs started to knock out the rats in no less than 1,860 villages.

Word of this feat at last cracked the resistance of the doubting farmers. Next, he and his AID colleagues taught the farmers how to deal with wheat smut; then seed cleaning and selection. Improved crops resulted. The specialists persuaded the farmers to cull some of their crowded fruit trees. They launched an attack on plant diseases, such as curly leaf, apple scab, and grape mildew. He helped to design a new kind of harness which enabled farmers to get more draft power from their horses.

Henry Botch was not particularly aware of anything unusual which he and his colleagues were doing. He was therefore taken completely by surprise one day when the local Iraqi postman handed him this letter:

DEAR MR. BOTCH:

When I was in Kirkuk, Iraq, this summer, I ran across your trail. I heard so many fine things about you that I thought I should write you that you left behind a host of friends who miss you very much and wish you well. In all my travels I have never run across the trail of anyone who was so universally praised.

The reports I got made me very anxious to meet you. . . .

I hope some day to meet you, and in any event, wanted to write you this note of appreciation for everything you have done for America in your fine service abroad.

Sincerely yours,
WILLIAM O. DOUGLAS
Justice of the Supreme Court

Land Reform

Of all the aspects of social and economic change with which foreign aid is concerned, the most controversial abroad and the least understood at home is land reform. It is also the one area where the U.S. must proceed with the utmost caution and tact, because in so many developing countries much of the land is still owned by a feudal few, who see the very mention of the word as an assault upon the status quo.

However, if nothing is done to make more land available to more people, the lot of the man at the bottom of the ladder worsens, while the pressure that can ultimately only explode in revolution builds up.

In actual fact, the term "land reform" includes various kinds of efforts to make land accessible to the tiller of the soil by any fair and equitable means. It does not necessarily entail expropriations, as many large landlords fear. Land reform can include renting on terms fair to both owner and tenant, the opening of new government lands where families can settle, or the purchase of large tracts with the subsequent sale of individual plots to farmers on easy terms.

In brief, land reform as viewed by AID fieldmen can follow three main approaches: Government land can be opened for settlement, as is being done in Brazil, the Philippines, Kenya, Bolivia, and several other countries.

Provisions may be made for improving landlord-tenant relations, such as guaranteeing tenants a fair share of the crop, occupancy rights, and compensation for improvements made on the land. This is the chief emphasis in India today. Tenants often prefer to rent good land from a just owner rather than to till poor land, perhaps the only kind they could afford.

Extremely large estates may be broken up, the government compensating the owner and reselling the land to farmers on long-term contracts. Where such lands were originally acquired justly, the landlord has no reason to fear. Indeed, the money a landlord gets for his land can usually earn a better return when invested elsewhere than was earned from the rent of their landholdings.

Serious situations prevail in many nations where excessive amounts of land have been acquired through conquest or oppression of the poor. However justly the present governments may move in reallocating the lands, the favored owners usually cry: "Communist!" or "expropriation!"

What can foreign aid do to encourage progress on this touchy but vital sector? Egypt offers an example of joint action by the United States and another country. I wanted to see for myself what was being accomplished, so on an early June morning in 1963, I met with Hussein El-Tahry, Director of Land Settlement in Egypt, at his Cairo office.

Hussein is an active, slender man of about forty years. On this Saturday morning he was in his shirt sleeves. When I came in, he was busy dispatching the last of several messengers. He rose to greet me. "Land settlement?" His face lighted up. "I'll be glad to give you whatever I can," he said. "Will you have a Coke?"

"No, thank you."

"Coffee?"

"Yes, please."

He beamed. "Ah, a real Egyptian!"

We sat down and he began to speak with warmth and vigor. "We have under way two approaches to the problem of land reform," he explained. "One is to divide up the large estates; the other is to reclaim unused land and to help resettle families. We are working very closely with your AID people in this." He handed me a booklet entitled

Egyptian-American Rehabilitation and Improvement Service.

"We refer to it as EARIS," he grinned. "Your alphabetical names even come here to perplex us. Here's how it works.

"On August 18, 1953, your government signed an agreement with us including these key points: To reclaim 42,500 acres of land, and to assist 8,000 landless families in getting settled on the reclaimed acreage; to make available for this purpose a joint fund of approximately $24 million, with the United Arab Republic guaranteeing 60 per cent, and your government, 40 per cent. Technicians are to be provided by both parties. Resettlement is to take place in three different areas, wherever we can get the best land. The work is to be administered by codirectors, Egyptian and American."

"Does Egypt have more land than what has already been staked out that could be reclaimed and settled?"

"Indeed, yes. We're a long country, you know, although we've become terribly narrow. The nation measures 750 miles from north to south. But the desert has edged in upon us so that on an average our tillable strip is no more than eight miles wide. We are not sure how far we can push back the desert, but estimates indicate that we have anywhere from 750,000 to 3 million acres that can be brought back into production. Believe me, we'll need every acre of it."

"On what basis did you select the 42,500 acres for settlement?"

"We make three simple tests: The land must be as near as possible to human habitation; there must be an ample source of water, either from wells or from irrigation, and the water must be reasonably salt-free; the chemical composition of the soil must measure up to satisfactory standards. These three form a kind of equation for our guidance."

"And the families—how are they chosen?"

"That's the heartbreaking part," he said, as his lean face grew solemn. "Put yourself in our position. You have perhaps a dozen five-acre farms and homes ready at a given time. To the landless, it's a paradise. As many as a hundred families apply for every home available. Most are worthy. They'll all work hard. They'll care for that land as if it were a member of the family. How would *you* decide?"

I had no answer.

"We've no recourse but to leave it up to a panel of judges. Oh, we can make a few rules that eliminate some," he continued. "For example, a man must be married and must be between the ages of twenty-one and forty. We give priority to applicants who have been farming successfully for at least ten years. We consider education too, although only a few of those who apply to us have had any schooling to speak of. We ask that they present a health certificate and character references.

"These are the rules. In the end, the judges can only hope they are doing the right thing. And, of course, there is the matter of need to be considered. We try to give preference to the largest families."

"What does a settler find when he arrives at his new home? What does it take to reclaim land?" I asked.

"It's no good merely sending people out to an empty place. They must find the essentials ready and waiting when they get there: water, a simple three-room house, roads, a school, health services, a cooperative store. Most of them come with no money, so a sum equal to about $105 is advanced to each family. Settlers contract to pay for the land and their house over a forty-year period. Each family starts out with a debt of $1,200."

"How many families do you find can be settled in a year?"

"In 1956, we settled the first eighty-eight families. Then it took us several years to acquire more land, to build roads, and the homes, and get everything ready. By last year, we had settled three thousand families. It ought to go faster now. But it's all so new and untried.

"We've been at it for ten years now, and we're not doing so badly. The pattern has been clarified. Before long, we should be clearing land and settling it at the rate of ten thousand or more families a year. We know now that land settlement is going to play a big part in Egypt's future.

I still find such men as El-Tahry incredible. Having only the most limited funds with which to work, and land that American farmers would scorn, he never doubts that because of this program, 500,000 families who are now homeless will see a better tomorrow.

Elsewhere in the world, particularly in Latin America, land reform is the demanding cry of millions. How this is to be accomplished depends upon proper planning and follow-up. Without careful preparation, things go wrong. Today, AID land economists are at work on plans which will help to pave the way toward orderly reform when it does come to Latin America. In Panama, a permanent team of land specialists has its headquarters. Members are available to make surveys and help in field plans as opportunities arise.

Land economists are currently working with the Brazilian Government on plans for a massive resettlement project. A tract of undeveloped land in the northwest is one of Brazil's great assets. At present, pilot settlements ranging from fifty to two hundred families are being made each year. AID provides assistance with advance surveys to determine which lands are most suitable. Studies are also made to determine what is known as the "pattern of migration." For example, can young couples be moved more successfully than older ones? Or, is a joint venture of several families or the movement of an entire community more likely to succeed?

"This may well be an important factor in both the political and economic future of that vast country," said a land specialist. "Indeed, the future of the Latin American continent may hinge on a few massive projects in each country carried out with imagination and thoroughness."

I have attempted to list only a few of the representative and more successful foreign aid achievements with which I happened to be personally familiar.

These, I grant, do not include a large number of projects in nonrural fields. There is no denying that there have been many mistakes, some of them costly. But are not some mistakes inevitable in any such large-scale enterprise that had to be so hastily developed?

At least, sufficient success has been achieved to assure us that the *job can and must be done*. Furthermore, we have experienced the satisfaction of alleviating some suffering and distress. The very doing of this may already have helped to determine the kind of world we will have in the future.

The outlook need not be gloomy. We see in it four threats and a challenge. The four threats are: rising hope which if unrecognized can reach revolutionary proportions; the widening gap between rich and poor; the mounting population curve; and the shame of hunger.

The challenge? Unlocking of the world's resources to meet human need.

As we look ahead, rather than despair over what we have failed to accomplish to date, we should try to see the future in larger perspective—to make an effort to understand the complexities; to make an effort to grasp the importance of U.S. foreign aid and its place in history.

In the next chapter, we will survey this job.

5

FOUR THREATS AND A CHALLENGE

NEARLY A hundred nations, a billion or more people wanting to rise from misery—the concept is almost staggering. In 1956, Dag Hammarskjöld said: "This will become the most challenging drama of all history." It is also the reason why we have foreign aid.

Rising Hope

I was traveling through Egypt with Yusaf Karim, a young officer from the Ministry of Agriculture. Near the bank of the Nile, we came upon a potter sitting cross-legged by his wheel, which spattered his white clothes with mud as he worked. He was turning out one perfect vessel after another with rhythmic precision. The potter, about sixty years of age, was lank and lean. With his gray beard, straggling gray hair, and sculptured face, he had the look of a philosopher.

A weary-looking woman, evidently his wife, came up from the river carrying a load of clay on her head and set it down beside him. A boy of about eighteen and a girl of ten assisted him. The boy carried water and mixed the clay with his feet, taking care to "wedge out" any bits of rock. The little girl deftly placed the soft clay pots in the sun to dry. Yusaf and I stood watching this efficient team. With a practiced gesture, the potter would grasp just the right amount of clay. In a moment, the little girl would come and take away the finished vessel.

"Your name?" I asked. My young guide, Yusaf Karim, interpreted for me.

"Kasum, just Kasum the potter," he replied.

"What do you earn, working like this all day, Kasum?"

"It is not so counted," he replied. He looked toward me for the first time. Only then did I notice he was blind.

"I work, then the broker comes, maybe tomorrow, maybe next week. I take what he gives me."

He gave the wheel a spin and went on forming more gray vessels, each one identical with the one before it. One-two-three-four, we watched and admired. He was turning out about fifteen vessels an hour. The little girl picked up each as it was done and hurried it away as if it were a precious treasure.

"It has always been so for me, and for those before me."

The wheel stopped. Kasum slowly straightened out his cramped legs. Finally he stood up, tall and slender, clay dripping from his hands. Looking far past us in the direction of the boy, through eyes that seemed to penetrate although they did not see, he said: "Take him, for example. He has new ideas. We know he may go to school.

"Above our heads we hear the planes—men fly with the birds. The radio tells us of green fields and places where food is plentiful. One day, no more of this for my son. Perhaps, not even for me. Tomorrow life will change. Today everyone hopes—it was never so before."

I was moved by his words. Before I could say anything, Kasum returned to his wheel. He gave it a vigorous spin and reached for a lump of clay.

Kasum's words echoed in my ears as I walked away: "Everyone hopes! It was never so before."

The potter spoke for his family and the little village where he lived. But he also spoke for all farm workers, unskilled laborers, the lowly ones in a hundred countries, who, like himself, were feeling new hope.

Only in this generation, for the first time, have they come to question what they had always believed—that their poverty had been ordained by fate. They are gaining confidence that they, too, can pull a lever, raise better crops, pass examinations, see a new world through a microscope.

In developing countries, a certain pattern of life is emerging. Raju Chotalal, whom I met in Central India, is typical of the small farmer in many regions. He is unable to do a proper day's work. His muscles are stringy because he has so long been underfed. His three-acre farm was taken from him by the moneylender to satisfy a debt.

Now he farms it as a tenant for a fourth of the crop. He is thirty-four, but he looks older. There is not much chance that he will live to reach the age which men in the West consider their prime.

Raju lives with his wife and five children in a one-room house made of earth, poles, and palm leaves. His wife cooks their one daily meal in a pot set on three stones. They have no electricity, no running water, no sanitary conveniences.

Raju himself cannot read or write. But it means a great deal to him that his older children, the ones who have clothes, can go to school. He is still in debt to the moneylender. Not in his lifetime will he be free; his son will inherit the debt. Because his strength has been sapped by sickness and lack of food, he cannot farm well. His wife works in the fields of others for three months of the year.

Ask the Rajus of this world what they want. They tell us without hesitation: food, clothing, medicine, education, justice. And the Rajus, with their families, make up nearly half the population of developing countries.

The new hope has fired the governments of some countries as well as the peasant farmers. Their officials are beginning to show an eagerness for improvement. In 1927, I was discussing soil conservation with a local agricultural officer in western India. I pointed to gullies which were widening with each monsoon and great areas where sheet erosion had done its work.

Casually he said: "You Westerners seem to be obsessed with soil erosion. As for us, we have no soil problems." I did not reply. He was right. They had no "soil problem" because erosion had already carried away the topsoil.

Last year, in that same area, I found farmers and government soil men busily at work plugging gullies and building barriers to check further erosion. It was the same land, but people were at work on it with a new vision, a new sense of urgency, striving to hold the creeping Rajputana Desert at bay while rebuilding the soil losses of centuries.

That was *their* expression of new hope.

We would be in error if we thought of the world situation only as the poor clamoring for bread, however badly bread is needed. Something greater is enshrined in this new hope. Those who listen to these people are impressed by the reasonableness of their demands. It is not power or riches that they seek, but education for their children, medical care, shelter, some land to till, or work for their hands. Above all is their passionate desire to be recognized, to achieve human dignity in the community of free nations.

These are people who, whether through isolation or oppression, were bypassed by the nineteenth-century revolutions in industry and agriculture, held back by tradition, by religious dogma, or by other inhibiting customs. Now, in a single stride, they hope to catch up with the twentieth century.

A generation ago this might have been a frightening prospect. Today it is within the realm of the possible! The world has the knowledge and technology to implement such an advance even though the fainthearted among us say with Hamlet:

> The time is out of joint; O cursed spite
> That I was ever born to set it right.

The fact that the job can be done does not in any way mean that it will be easy. As David Bell warns: "Rapid population growth, Communist subversion, repressive military dictatorships, poverty, and ignorance will not be overcome overnight." * But to the enterprising, this is an era of challenge and hope. The prospects for advance are promising. The possibilities for agriculture, commerce, and industry can all be enormous if we but apply with determination and skill the technology of which we are now masters.

The Widening Gap

A new element must be taken into consideration: the widening gap in the level of living between the "have" and the "have-not" countries. We speak politely of the developed and the underdeveloped countries.

Barbara Ward, the British author on economics, more precisely refers to them as the rich nations and the poor nations. Bluntly she warns us the rich nations are getting richer, the poor nations, poorer.†

This widening gap was the gloomiest specter which haunted the Geneva Conference on Trade and Commerce in the spring and summer of 1964.

To advance, a country must first either grow a sufficient amount of food, or produce enough goods to be exchanged for that food. The developing countries as a rule are unable to do either. Facts brought out at the conference showed we are growing closer together in communication, but farther and farther apart economically and ideologically.

Once we could take refuge in what Gunnar Myrdal called "the convenience of ignorance." ‡ We could ignore famine, economic oppression, and hunger because they were happening to people whom we did not know in remote parts of the world.

But speed of travel, equal membership in the U.N., and such revolutionary devices in communication as Telstar have cleared the fog. The Korean farmer, the Thai craftsman, and the Andean shepherd are now our neighbors. We

* *Christian Science Monitor,* January 15, 1964.

† Barbara Ward, *The Rich Nations and the Poor Nations* (New York: Norton, 1962), p. 3.

‡ Gunnar Myrdal, *Rich Lands and Poor* (New York: Harper and Row, 1957), p. 72.

trade on all continents; we exchange news minute by minute; we travel around the world in a matter of hours.

What do the figures tell us about this widening gap? The most reliable index we have is per capita income. It is calculated by dividing a nation's capital income by its population.

On this basis, the peoples of the developing world had an income of $88 per person in 1951. By 1961, after ten years of intensive effort, the figure had risen to a bare $98, an increase at the rate of one dollar a year. During the same period, the people of Western Europe had an increase equivalent to $27.50; in the United States, the per capita annual income increased by $225.*

If we, as of today, consider the per capita income of Asia in relationship to other areas of the world, the comparison looks like this: †

Asia	1
Latin America	2
World Average	5
Western Europe	11
United States	31

Estimates of this kind have their limitations. But their relative differences tell their own story of why one-half of the world is so determined to achieve a better life.

Within poor countries, too, the gap between its own rich and poor is often out of all proportion. In lands where government is controlled by a privileged elite, such economic expansion as does occur is likely to do so largely in luxury products and services for those already well-to-do.

India has made a serious effort to distribute income and services fairly. Yet a member of the Agricultural Planning Committee told me: "I am deeply concerned that perhaps one-fourth of our people have not bettered their lot economically by our First and Second Five-Year Plans. Infla-

* *Facts about Economic Growth and Development* (Washington, D.C.: Center for International Economic Growth, 1957).

† Justin Roe Nixon, *Man's New Hope* (New York: Church Peace Union, 1957), p. 13.

tionary food prices, uneven distribution of income, and population increase are pushing down the level of living for many to below what it was at the start."

Paul G. Hoffman, Director of the U.N. Special Fund says: "Results from our first ten years of effort are far from satisfying." *

There are several reasons for the stubborn persistence of this gap in income between poor and rich countries. The economic health of many nations depends on the export of raw materials, including lumber, ores, jute, or such agricultural products as coffee, cocoa, fruit, or rubber. Because of differences in exchange, the prices received are often low compared to the prices they must pay for machines needed to increase production. Some have no capital with which to develop industry. Others lack natural resources such as coal, oil, or other mineral wealth.

The Middle Eastern and North African countries long ago lost their soil through erosion and therefore have few agricultural products to export. Much of the potential farmland of Africa and parts of Latin America is either desert or badly leached rain forest, capable of producing crops only after the investment of large sums of money. And always, everywhere, is the shortage of skilled manpower.

Barbara Ward reasons:

> It is very much easier for a rich man to invest and grow than for the poor man to begin investing at all. And this is also true of nations. The new world is not yet born. This being so, the gap between the rich and the poor has become inevitably the most tragic and most urgent problem of our day.†

Mounting Population

Prior to 1950, in most developing countries, disease, in its cruel but effective way, kept population in balance with

* Paul G. Hoffman, *Freedom From Want* (New York: Harper and Row, 1962), pp. 66 ff.

† *Op. cit.*, pp. 35–36.

the food supply. Famines did their deadly work, those of the 1940's killing between 2 and 3 million people in East India alone. Such mass killers as malaria, typhus, cholera, and other plagues carried on their slaughter unimpeded. Local governments, church and welfare organizations counterattacked to the limit of their abilities. But they did not have the resources to deal with diseases on a mass scale.

Then came the miracle drugs and new insecticides developed during World War II. In WHO, the World Health Organization of the United Nations, assisted by public health departments, an instrumentality came into being to put the new discoveries to use on a scale unknown before.

The average life span in some of the countries once heavily afflicted by disease has already been lengthened considerably. In India, for example, life expectancy has increased from twenty-seven years to forty. Infant mortality has been reduced in some countries by as much as one-half. One cannot but hail these advances in medicine, for they have brought not only a longer but a happier and richer life to millions.

But in alleviating one critical problem, the world has been presented with another, perhaps even more critical. A growth in population has taken place which is unprecedented in human history. Agriculture, by failing to produce miracles comparable to those of medicine, has been unable to bring about an increase in food to eat which is equal to the increased rate of mouths that must be fed. In the twenty minutes it takes to read this chapter, nearly 1,200 additional mouths have added their hungry plea for food.

Ironically enough, it is in the poorest countries that the population rise is fastest. Among its other effects, the increase also cuts down the amount of cropland available per person. In 1925, India had a meager 1.1 acres of cropland per person. Three years later, the India Famine Commission reported that under conditions of good husbandry there should be a minimum of 1.4 acres of cropland per person. Today, in spite of heroic efforts in land reclamation over the last decade, the available cropland per person has declined to .8 acre.

In the twenty-two Asian countries that stretch from Iran to Japan, population is growing four times as fast as the food supply, according to recent figures compiled by the United Nations. Their 1963–64 survey shows population of those countries mounting at the rate of 2.4 per cent per year; the per capita food supply is trailing behind at an increase of .5 per cent per year.

Rates of population increase are the highest in Latin America where the Catholic Church has traditionally opposed restricting the number of children by "unnatural" means. While India is becoming alarmed over her present population increase of 2.2 per cent per year, Costa Rica, El Salvador, and Mexico have reached yearly growth rates of approximately 3.4 per cent. Such increases create demands for housing, education, and food which would be a difficult burden for any country to bear, even one with a high standard of living.

Thirty-five years ago, Mahatma Gandhi, moving among the peasants of India, called hunger the "eternal compulsory fast." India must now plan on feeding 8 million new mouths every year, an annual increase equal to the total population of New York City. In Calcutta alone, more than 200,000 people live, eat, sleep, and die on the streets.

Similar conditions are developing in Jakarta, Seoul, and Rio de Janeiro, where housing and employment are rapidly falling behind population increase. The number keeps on growing despite efforts of officials to find homes and jobs for those flocking in from the villages.

Delegates from 110 countries meeting in Washington, D.C., in June, 1963, to recommend a course of action to take in view of rapid population growth and world hunger were appalled to hear that every day 10,000 people are starving to death.

Stony silence greeted the statements that despite major efforts, food production is not keeping pace with population growth. One-third of the world's people still go to bed hungry. Addressing the conference, President Kennedy warned: "The war against hunger is truly mankind's war of liberation. There is no battle on earth or in space more important for peace. Progress cannot be maintained in a world half-fed and half-hungry."

To win the battle against hunger, the growth of population must be slowed down and the production of food speeded up. This sounds staggering, but it is not impossible. We see a shaft of light in Japan, where a reduction in the birthrate from 2 per cent to 1 per cent a year has been achieved over the past fifteen years. India has made a start, with a decline in births from 48 per thousand in 1931 to 40 per thousand at the close of the Second Five-Year Plan in 1961. More than 8,240 family planning clinics are now in operation, but results will take time. Alas, so far, none of the other developing countries has made a beginning.

Historian Arnold Toynbee warned: "Mankind's future is at stake in a formidable race between population growth and famine." * This same warning now comes from Raymond Ewell, Vice President for Research, State University of New York: †

> The world is on the threshold of the greatest famine in history on the three continents of Asia, Africa, Latin America. If present trends continue, it seems likely that famine will reach serious proportions in India, Pakistan, and China in the 1970's —then followed by most of the countries of Asia, Africa, and Latin America. Such a famine will be of massive proportions, affecting hundreds of millions.

He concludes that there are two ways out: 1) Immediate steps for population control; 2) Increasing world food production.

The World Food Basket

Up to the present moment in the world's history, there have not only been far fewer people to feed, but much more abundant resources on which to draw. Man was always opening up new lands, or pushing farther out upon the

* An address delivered before the World Food Congress, Washington, D.C., June 14–18, 1963.

† An address before the American Chemical Society, Chicago, September, 1964.

oceans for better fishing grounds, or seeking the undiscovered country. Today, we face an unprecedented demand for food with far fewer frontiers open to us.

Such estimates as "more than half the world goes to bed hungry" or "half the babies born in poor countries die from hunger before they reach the age of six"—are they accurate? How can they be measured?

The quality and types of food vary from country to country. We have only limited data as to the amount of leaves, nuts, and other native foods gathered by peasant peoples. Nor do we have enough information concerning the relationship between climate and the number of calories required for adequate nutrition. Ironically, we seem to possess far more precise data with respect to space travel than we do with respect to the much more urgent problem of world hunger. We do know the number of calories available to people of a given country. Although this is not a precise measure, it is the best yardstick we have.

The experience of the British has given us our most complete information on this subject. During World War II, it was discovered that when the adult diet for active workers dropped to 2,800 calories per day, efficiency began to be impaired.*

What do we find if we apply this calorie yardstick to the world as a whole? Only about one-fifth of the world's people enjoy a diet of as much as 2,800 calories a day. And most of them are in the developed countries of the West.

Daily food intake for the people of the developing countries, who account for over 60 per cent of the world's population, is under 2,200 calories. For over one-half of these, the diet falls below 2,000 calories. Thus, the frequently heard statement that nearly one-half the world is presently suffering from malnutrition and hunger has sound basis in fact.

Nutritionists remind us of a mistaken idea abroad to the effect that people in warmer climates require far fewer

* Dr. Norman C. Wright, *Hunger* (London: British Association for the Advancement of Science, 1962), p. 2.

calories than those in the temperate zones. There is a difference, due to milder climate, especially among those who have sedentary employment. However, the large number of people in these countries engaged in long hours of severe physical labor should have perhaps as many calories as people in the temperate zones whose labor is lightened by the machine and who use very few calories in walking. The peasant laborer who wields the pickax or the spade from daylight to dark probably needs nearly as many food calories as the workman in the West, whose heaviest work is done by machines.

The developed countries can think of food in terms other than survival. Partaking of it in variety can be a source of daily pleasure. Mealtimes are an occasion for pleasant fellowship. To the rest of the world, to eat is to take in just enough fuel to maintain existence. Those who suffer most from starvation speak of it as "belly fire" because of the gnawing pains hunger produces as the stomach shrivels and the body slowly devours itself.

Famine, when it occurs on a large scale, is usually dramatic enough to assure the taking of relief measures. But hunger, slow starvation, is a different matter. Its anguish goes on year after year, until the time comes when, as Seneca warned the fat statesmen of Rome 1,900 years ago: "A hungry people listens not to reason nor is its demand turned aside by prayers."

Loss of weight and retarded growth are the first visible effects. Then come mental dullness, lassitude, fatigue, and weakness. Employers in the countries ridden by hunger often have to provide their employees with a noonday meal as part of the wage in order for laborers to have strength to work.

In the healthy countries of the West, starchy grains such as wheat, corn, and rice make up no more than one-fourth of the diet, whereas in Asia, Latin America, and Africa, starches such as cassava root, maize, and polished rice constitute nearly 80 per cent.

Skin sores, blindness, pellagra, anemia, and kwashiorkor

are the results of dietary deficiencies. Dr. Hazel E. Hauck, nutritionist of Cornell University, found that "very few children in West Africa escape the deformities of kwashiorkor that result from a high starch diet." Those who travel in Asian countries are familiar with the bloated stomachs of hungry children. But these are only the most spectacular of the many diseases caused by dietary imbalance.

Scientists attending the Symposium on Hunger held at Cardiff, Wales, in 1960, noted: "From a *technical standpoint* world hunger need not be feared for at least forty years." They agreed that by full use of our present knowledge and resources, sufficient food could be produced. However, the Symposium agreed that increased production could not be achieved with anything short of the prompt and full mobilization of *all* of our resources. Nor did the delegates overlook the fact that hunger in grave proportions already exists.

Hunger is no longer a mere abstract problem to be discussed statistically, in academic terms. It is a gruesome specter haunting us today, a monster that in the near future could destroy the human race by setting man against man. We are told by experts that if the rapidly growing world population is to be fed, food production must be doubled by the year 1980.

It puzzles people of hungry countries to see us complacently deploying our best scientists and ten times the amount we spend on aid to place men on the moon. The planet earth is still like Mother Hubbard with only a bare cupboard for one-third of her people. Surely we are not going to find an answer to this, our foremost problem, awaiting us on the moon!

What Science Can Offer

The world's food picture is far from hopeless. In spite of serious obstacles, there is much that can be done, if we understand the necessity and have the will to attack the problem.

Most agronomists agree that the first step in getting more food is to help farmers cut the losses incurred on crops they are already producing. FAO workers maintain that even with all our chemical advances, plant diseases and insects today are still destroying one-fourth of the world's food before it reaches the storage bins. Once farmers were helpless and could only look on in despair as these unchecked forces of nature laid waste their crops in the field or ruined vast amounts of precious grain in their bins.

Now, thanks to chemicals and better means for storage, these losses can be greatly reduced. Experiments have shown that $2.00 spent for the control of rust and smut in grain will save up to a ton of food.

In the Philippines and elsewhere, the ordinary field rat is still a potent foe to farmers. The rodents hide in hedges, and then they advance in hordes to devour the ripening ears of corn or gnaw rice plant roots. Farmers try to frighten them away with rocks and shouts, but the devastation goes on. This loss could soon be eliminated altogether if we but used the chemicals and technical weapons at our command on a large scale.

Fertilizers, as noted above, are generally recognized as the first step to increase yields from worn-out soils. Yet their proper use in developing countries is still to begin. We have no world shortage of raw materials. The supply of nitrogen from the air is almost unlimited. Geologists calculate that known deposits of potash and phosphate rock are adequate to last from three to five thousand years. The task of preparing and delivering this material where it can be utilized is far from simple, and as yet less than 1 per cent of the fertilizer needed is available. Among the developing countries, only three or four have made any beginning on plans to manufacture and use fertilizers.

Much can be done to increase yields by improving varieties of crops. Potatoes are an example. Only a generation ago, U.S. farmers were pleased to get 80 bushels from an acre; now they expect at least 200 bushels. Yields of 500 bushels per acre are common. Until 1952, it was thought potatoes could not be grown extensively in India because of the climate. Now, through the introduction of new varieties and new fertilizers, they are grown widely; farms in the Ganges Valley, one of the country's hottest areas, are yielding as much as 400 bushels an acre.

England has come forward with a revolutionary growing method. Farmers place the seed potatoes on top of the ground and cover them with strips of the plastic, black polyethylene. Cross-shaped cuts are made to let the potato stalks come through. At harvest time, the farmer simply rolls back the cover and picks up clean tubers. This method, as reported, has brought about a 25 per cent increase in yield.

The world average for wheat yield is just under 11 bushels per acre. While not all soils and climates are equally productive, yields up to 60 bushels per acre are now realized over large areas of the Western world and Japan. Some yields much larger than this are known. But we were all inclined to cheer in October, 1964, when the *Farm Journal* reported that Otis Helsley, a farmer in Grant County, Washington, produced a yield of 168 bushels per acre on a twenty-six acre field! To achieve this miraculous result he used a new, stumpy variety that permits many more stalks per acre. The new variety, known so far only as "shorty," does not "lodge" readily or fall to the ground under the effects of heavy doses of fertilizer and irrigation.

Corn yields of 100 bushels per acre are now common, with yields of over 300 bushels achieved on specially treated fields. The average yield of corn for the U.S. has jumped more than 100 per cent, from 28.8 bushels per acre in 1940, to 63 in 1964. The state average for Indiana is 88 bushels.

Soybeans have recently become recognized as a food crop of world importance. In 1930, American farmers were happy to get 28 bushels per acre; today, with fertilizer and improved varieties, yields of 40 bushels are common.

Equally important results are being achieved with animals and poultry in the production of meat, eggs, and milk. For example, the number of eggs per hen has tripled since 1910, while the quality has been improved.

Obviously these results cannot be expected in all areas of the world. Nor can they be expected within a short time. But they do indicate some of the possibilities that science can offer.

The world is no longer the immense unknown that it once was. We can examine it, and its problems at least are made comprehensible. Thirty years ago we would not have known how to feed the world of today. Now we do at least have the technical resources at our command. Is it too optimistic to believe that we will find ways for putting our immense technical resources to work on a world scale before it is too late?

The Farmer Holds the Key

Food production with limited land resources has already become an art and a science in some countries—notably Japan, Denmark, Belgium, and Holland, for example. Many facets are to be considered, but in the end, it is the farmer who holds the key.

Although farms vary widely as to size and methods of operation, all farmers have one thing in common: they are producers of food and fiber. Farming, unlike most other economic enterprises, is dispersed among millions of small family units. A few factories can make the tractors or automobiles we use, but the world's food is grown on more than 300 million farms, many of them under five acres.

Farms will continue to become larger as mechanization is adopted, and no doubt thousands of the less efficient farmers will be squeezed out. But even so, for generations to come, the world's food will be produced on millions of family farms. It is easy to overlook the farmer in our conference-table discussions about foreign aid. Yet it is he to whom we must chiefly look to grow the extra food that is essential to feed the increasing multitudes.

Reports of record crop yields are universally exciting. But

so far, these records remain the achievements of no more than a handful of the world's farmers. In Western countries it is easy for technology to be widely disseminated. The farmer is within access of improved roads. Skilled and experienced counsel, moreover, is readily available to him. In one Illinois county for example, 2,400 farmers have eight extension agents to assist them.

By way of contrast, I met an agricultural agent in Nigeria last year who had responsibility for advising 21,000 farmers. Of these, 80 per cent were illiterate; no more than a handful lived along highways. The others were scattered in villages accessible only by foot trails.

The men who work the small, remote farms will do their proportionate part to fill up the world's food basket. But it is up to the developed countries to see that they get their chance.

There was a time when we could take comfort in quoting out of context the biblical phrase: "For you have the poor always with you." Problems of poverty, oppression, even hunger, could be looked at with complacency because we had neither the skill, the knowledge, nor the means to do anything about them. We could afford to ignore these discomfiting situations elsewhere in the world because they were only smoldering. Today they are ablaze!

6

WHY PROGRESS IS SLOW

When Point Four was announced that bright January day in 1949, many Americans had high hopes that it would take no more than a few years for our technology to bring new life to suffering peoples. The success of the Marshall Plan led some to think that our obligation to developing countries might even be discharged within one Presidential term.

But fourteen years have gone by, and thoughtful observers tell us that we may as well expect to go on supporting foreign aid for another twenty years at best; and perhaps, if we are realistic, for the rest of this century.

The first flush of enthusiasm has paled. Many are asking: "Why is progress so slow? Why can't such a simple matter as hunger be alleviated more quickly? Where is our technology?"

No one can give a pat answer to these questions. But a close view of situations in developing lands can help us understand why foreign aid has not been able to move any faster toward its goals.

Most of us are aware of certain obvious roadblocks, such

as the population explosion and illiteracy. But other less well-known obstacles are seldom considered by the critics of foreign aid. Thirty-five years of experience with this and closely related endeavors has focused my thoughts upon the following eight propositions.

The Great Unknown

One day in 1820, in a trading post on Mackinac Island, a shotgun went off, wounding a North American Indian, Alexis St. Martin. The shot tore away the muscles of his abdomen, exposing the outer wall of his stomach. William Beaumont, a young surgeon stationed near the trading post, with great difficulty and much pain to the patient, stitched together the edges of the muscles and skin. St. Martin recovered, but he was left with a "window" through which Dr. Beaumont could observe the stomach at work. St. Martin lived as a handyman with the doctor for many years, during which time Dr. Beaumont recorded his observations on the digestive process. Dr. Beaumont then wrote a book about what he had learned, which became a significant contribution to medical science.

Even though we may have had various "windows" on the developing world by means of study, travel, and radio, we have not used them as did the observant Dr. Beaumont. So when we began the exacting foreign aid assignment, too many of us were like the blind man who could only "feel" the elephant. We had to proceed largely by trial and error.

We can now see that economic growth is no simple process requiring only handy injections of technical knowledge and capital to speed it up. Our early technicians suffered grievous handicaps because they had prepared for their assignments under one set of ideas and objectives, while the people they hoped to emancipate were held back by entirely different circumstances. We have indeed made progress. But we have yet to learn how best to work with peoples of other races and alien cultures.

Even with our Latin American neighbors, there has been lack of understanding. Three times we have found it necessary to reorganize the Alliance for Progress, formulated in 1961. As a nation of wealth and power, we have found it hard to overcome what some call the "illusion of our omnipotence." Some of us are unable to approach people of other lands without appearing to patronize them. This is particularly hurtful in countries which are still smarting from the sting of colonial domination. We have still to realize that however poor a nation may be, no *man* considers himself underdeveloped!

I cannot forget what a wise agronomist in West Pakistan said to me in the summer of 1963: "Any gesture of aid at all gives us hope. But if your technicians are to be of enduring help to us, they must learn to stand in our shoes and see the problems from our point of view.

"Consider for a moment how different is our situation from your own. For one thing, our deprived population is enormous. We have no great plains suitable for homesteading. Our frontiers are sandy wastelands which need to be reclaimed acre by acre. Your men puzzle us when they speak zealously of *your* technology and *our* needs. Yes, we need help desperately, but we must have those who can identify themselves with us and our situation."

Variations of Nature

One powerful force impeding the pace of our efforts is Mother Nature herself. From the romantic accounts of traveling writers, or writing travelers, one may get an impression of vast areas of the earth awaiting only the touch of the technologist to bring them into bloom.

This concept is deceptive. Empty areas exist, to be sure. But they are often too hot or too cold, too dry or too wet for productive farming. Sarawak and Sierra Leone, for example, have over 200 inches of rainfall annually; other parts of the earth have little or none. Much of North Africa and the Near East is desert. Such lands can be redeveloped, but it will take a lot of time and money.

The British have given independence to West Africa, but the tsetse fly still holds sway over millions of acres of land, infecting both man and cattle, thus making modern farming extremely difficult. New drugs are being tested, but as yet no broadly effective remedy is in sight.

Engineers sometimes develop irrigation works under the most trying conditions, only to encounter new problems: water logging, for example, or the rise of alkaline salts in the soil, or porous bottoms in reservoir areas.

Many developing lands are tropical, with a ten-to-twelve month growing season. This sounds promising, but it often proves a liability as well as an asset. The winter freeze helps to keep down soil bacteria, insects, and plant diseases in colder countries. In hot, humid areas there is no such climatic check.

In the rain forests, if fertilizers are added to the soil, the heavy downpours leach them away. In other areas, high temperatures burn up soil humus in no time. An agricultural missionary in Ghana said to me: "A New York dairy farm set up here, and operated as it is at home, would be leached out by rain and burned up from heat and bacteria within five years."

Scientists are working on these problems, but we must give them time. Some day, with their help, what are now the jungles and deserts of the world may be producing wonders in food and fiber.

Mineral resources are yet to be exploited in some developing nations. For centuries, potentates of the Near East sat cross-legged in their tents above rich reservoirs of oil without knowing it, while their people starved. Latin America and parts of Africa are rich in mineral resources, but means for refining and transporting them must be developed. Hardwood forests cover remote parts of Africa and the eastern slopes of the Andes, but roads must be built so the logs can be hauled out.

Handicaps of Tradition

In certain instances, culture traits retard progress. Reliance on magic and adherence to ancient tribal customs still hold back much of Africa. Allocation of land to tribes rather than to individuals or families often results in indifferent husbandry and low crop yields, for no one feels personal responsibility.

In Afghanistan, since early history, certain public lands have been set aside for the grazing of sheep and cattle. But continued grazing has resulted in inferior grass and shrubs of little use to anyone. Foreign aid workers were assigned to help improve these pasture lands. However, before they could plant seed, they had to build fences, clear away rocks and brush, and temporarily restrict grazing. It took a lot of persuasion to get the herdsmen to relinquish grazing privileges for a while, even though it was for their future benefit. It took, in fact, five years!

In much of the world, those who have gone through college still consider it beneath their dignity to work with their hands. Law schools, medical schools, and liberal arts colleges are overcrowded, while trade schools cannot fill their rolls. A white-collar job is still considered the highest prize by those who have managed to get beyond the elementary grades. This brings about an exodus of the educated from the villages, resulting in congestion, unemployment, and unrest in the cities. Rural areas are left short of trained leaders.

This attitude toward what is regarded as menial work is finally beginning to change, but it will be years before we see widespread acceptance of the blue-collar job.

The yearning for progress in any given underdeveloped country is not shared by all classes, by any means. The wealthy landowners usually resist change which does not benefit them. In many countries, particularly in Latin America, life is organized according to a pattern of privilege. The rich, theoretically, are endowed with status they have inherited at birth, along with their lands. It is similarly assumed that the poor are born to their lot of privation and drudgery. If they are in want, so the comfortable like to think, it is largely because they are lazy, inept, and shiftless.

However unjustly the title to land may have been acquired in the past, it is automatically passed along from one generation to the next as a matter of inherent right. Political position is often dependent upon land holdings and social status. Politicians as a class admit that they do not intend to risk their careers by endorsing economic or social reforms that might prove unpopular with those at the top of the social ladder.

This resistance becomes adamant wherever such issues as land reform or tax increases are pressed. The well-to-do generally are not disposed to tax themselves voluntarily or to give up a way of life that is economically profitable, politically advantageous, and socially pleasant.

Privilege also dictates the order of things in universities and colleges. The university curriculum is often designed largely to serve the requirements of an elite. However, in much of Africa and in some countries of Asia, steps are being taken to correct this condition.

In many countries, civil service in itself has become an entrenchment of privilege. The government is packed with office holders who contribute little or nothing. Many cooperative societies in underdeveloped countries are not serving the people, because supervising officers are either too busy or not qualified to aid the people in establishing themselves from the ground up.

Resistance from a privileged class constitutes one of the most formidable obstacles to economic change. It limits the amount of aid that can be productively put to work, and deprives the poor of the help they need and deserve. Many of our foreign aid officers are too soft or inexperienced in dealing with this resistance from the privileged elite. We must find ways for more boldly channeling aid directly to the poor, or our money and efforts will continue to be wasted.

Peasant farmers, too, while eager to have their old wrongs righted, show their conservative side when any change is suggested in the traditional way of doing things. This attitude is not always a liability. It protects the farmer against the havoc that might result from a host of untested ideas and assures the continuity of at least a modest, if precarious existence. For generations, armed only with the hoe and the machete, these men of the soil have held their own against the rigors of nature. Living at the edge of want, their reluctance to take any jump in the dark is understandable.

I have walked miles with the farmers of the Near East and Asia, guiding the wooden plow while the farmer drove the oxen. I have come to have great admiration for their courage, stamina, and ability to make the most out of little. Who among us in the West could take a hoe, a wooden plow, a yoke of half-starved beasts, a few patches of depleted soil, and undertake to eke out survival for a family?

Peasant farming is deeply rooted in religion, family ties, tradition, and beliefs developed over thousands of years. Changes must and will come, but the adviser must be able to suggest methods that have been tested and proved under similar conditions. The farmer is eager to find his way to a better life. But it is he who takes the risk on the new ideas, not the adviser, whose livelihood is not contingent on the success of what he recommends.

We find it hard to imagine people living on the soil who are without food. Yet most of the peasant farmers of the world are underfed. When they have paid the usurer and the landlord, little is left from their meager crops for themselves. Simple hunger is the obvious cause of what is often described as their "lethargy" or their "apathy" in the face of proffered change.

Under the Marshall Plan, the first $2 billion grant distributed was earmarked to feed the factory workers until the products could come rolling off the assembly line. Perhaps our "grow more food programs" would meet with greater success, if we started by seeing that the peasant farmer, his wife and family, and his livestock were decently fed, before we flooded him with advice.

Without the motivating force of national pride, no country can become strong. But the excessive pride of political leaders is preventing some countries today from seeking the very technical and economic aid necessary for their progress.

It is quite natural that the long fight to escape from colonial rule, followed by the sudden achievement of freedom, should leave these new governments imbued with a deep suspicion when offered help from outside.

This pride sometimes reaches proportions of bitterness, as in the case of some African countries. As they now try to rebuild, they find that much of their resources—iron, copper, ivory, rubber, and timber—have been wasted and even hauled off wholesale by exploiting traders during colonial times.

The same anger mitigates against the acceptance of foreign technical advisers, however badly they may be needed.

Land Is Gold

One of the hotly disputed bars to progress in foreign aid is the shortage of good land. A farmer requires a large land surface on which to produce his crops. I once talked with a miller in India who said he was grinding 42,000 bushels of wheat into flour each year with a small mill that occupied a space of land only 20 by 30 feet. I was astonished when I estimated that no less than 2,000 acres of land had been needed to grow the wheat.

In the United States, homesteading is imbedded in our history. The government's practice of allotting generous tracts of land—usually 160 acres—for a nominal sum to anyone willing to live on it has continued into recent years. Today, with surplus land and surplus crops, we spend over $1 billion per year on a program to pay farmers for not planting some of their land.

It is difficult for many of us, reared in such a tradition, to understand what ownership, or at least the use of land, can mean to those who live deprived of it, in crowded countries, often under the heel of oppression.

While we think of Africa as a continent of unlimited land resources, an acute shortage has already developed in such countries as Kenya, Nigeria, and Rhodesia, where as many as 1,150 Africans are crowded into one square mile.

This peasant attitude toward land was brought home to

me several years ago when I was in India. Two farmers called upon me one afternoon to arbitrate a dispute concerning the placement of a line fence between two fields. The controversy concerned a strip of land only five inches wide. One, a Muslim, said: "This land is of gold. Allah himself gave it to my forefathers."

The other, equally inflexible, insisted the five precious inches were his. I had lived in India long enough to understand how passionately each felt about the ownership of even so tiny a strip of earth. To achieve the logical compromise—which was to persuade each to yield half—took all the tact I could muster and more time than I had to spare.

Peasant people the world over, so I have learned, will pay any price, will make any sacrifice to get land of their own to till. The fellahs of Egypt like to be known as the "sons of the black earth." The Japanese have a saying to this effect: "A farmer without land is a body without a soul."

Indians of the Andes, who are descended from the proud Incas, still mourn the loss of their land to the Spanish conqueror, after centuries.

The Nigerians give perhaps the most eloquent tongue to this respect for land, in their adage: "The land belongs to a vast family, of which many are dead, a few are living, and countless numbers are still to be born." *

It is even hard to make a first move toward change until something can be done about the use of land. Naturally, the large landlord who controls most of the productive soil in developing countries values his holdings. To him, they represent not only a cherished form of wealth, but social prestige and control over the tenants who occupy them. Land ownership goes hand in hand with political power.

Not all landlords can be condemned out of hand. Whenever one of them takes an interest in community affairs, and many do, his power can be highly beneficial. Tenants under well-disposed patrons may be better off economically than

* Laslim Olawalde Elias, *Nigerian Law and Land Custom* (2nd ed.; London: Routledge and Kegan Paul Ltd.), p. 153.

on the little plots of second-rate land which they could afford. But beyond question, development in much of the world is seriously retarded by a feudalistic system of large holdings whose owners have little concern for the advancement of the country as a whole. Latin America offers us a vivid example.

This concentrated form of land holding became firmly rooted there in 1529, when Hernando Cortez received a grant of 100,000 Indians and 25,000 square miles of land from the King of Spain. Possession of this type of holding or latifundium includes the peon families as well as the buildings, fences, and trees. Today, over three-fourths of the tillable land of Latin America is held by 6 per cent of the people.

What is the land situation in representative underdeveloped nations of the world?

The 1961 Report of the Food and Agriculture Organization of the United Nations suggests 1.5 acres of good cropland as the minimum per person to maintain nutrition and afford a decent standard of living. Circumstances such as climate, rainfall, and quality of the soil must be taken into consideration; but on the basis of 1.5 acre minimum, the people of many countries are suffering under land shortage. Here are some examples:

Country	*Acres of Cropland per Person*
Egypt	.2
India	.8
Japan	.2
Java	.3
South Korea	.5

By way of comparison, Canada has four acres of cropland per person; the United States, three; New Zealand, four. Land, of course, varies greatly in productivity.

Most developing countries have at least undertaken some sort of land reform. Mexico, beginning with the Revolution in 1910, has probably gone farthest. In the Philippines, the program of resettlement President Magsaysay started has been allowed to slow down. Egypt made spectacular strides in breaking up large estates, then slowed to a halt when most of the available land had been redistributed. At present there is little more to parcel, until irrigation projects now under construction have been completed.

A most recent and hopeful reform is to be tried in Peru, where, as noted in the first chapter, years of political bickering have delayed a necessary reapportionment of land. Now, at last, a settlement may be reached, and without the dreaded bloodshed and Communist takeover. The large, highly mechanized coastal sugar plantations, the efficiently run livestock ranches remain as they are. But haciendas of 3,000 acres and up, which are at present uncultivated or unproductive, are to be purchased by the government at a fair market value. On this land, 1 million farmers—now landless—will be settled and allotted parcels varying from 32 acres in rich coastal areas to 75 acres in the highlands. In order to avoid repeating past mistakes, separate agencies are to be set up which will offer credit and technical assistance. Other countries are watching this long-delayed endeavor with interest.

Bolivia's first efforts at land reform, begun in 1952, ended chaotically. Acreage was merely parceled out to Indians without any follow-up counsel or financial assistance, always so necessary until the first crops are produced.

Egypt, on the other hand, was able to avert such a disaster by providing farm advisers and cooperative marketing and credit societies for the new owners. The subject of land reform still propounds many baffling questions: How far, for example, should a country go in breaking up large estates into small farms? Western economists deplore the very small farm as being uneconomical. But to what extent can this purely economic concept be applied to densely populated areas, with their multitudes of unemployed clamoring for land, however small the plots may be? How far can it be applied to areas such as Nigeria or Egypt where possession of land has such profound social and cultural connotations?

Controversy continues in India where perhaps the most ambitious land reform legislation of modern times remains on dead center, while landlords oppose and the amount of land to be allocated per person is disputed. Obviously various circumstances have to be considered: the kind of land, type of farming, whether it is to be irrigated or not. Each province has its own particular problems to solve.

Some Indian leaders want the ceiling, the maximum amount an individual can hold, to be large enough to employ two workers, even a tractor. Members of the Land Reforms Committee who hold this view say: "Tiny farms are wasteful because the same amount of money invested in oxen and equipment can till twenty acres as well as five acres."

Claimants for lower ceilings contend: "The peasant hungers for land just as he does for food and water. No one should be allowed to have excess at the expense of others. Land hunger must be satisfied by giving the peasants land in howsoever small plots."

Leaders in some countries despair of achieving land reform at all, short of violent and possibly totalitarian change. But Wolfe Ladejinsky, U.S. agricultural adviser who has given a lifetime to land reform work in a dozen different countries, has declared: "The land problem *can* be dealt with resolutely without the Communist gospel of tragic upheavals."

Any land reform, particularly a redistribution which tries to be fair, takes time, entailing as it does basic alteration of the status quo. But until reform is brought about, the total program of development is retarded. Landlords who have sold their land and invested the proceeds in industry have often found themselves better off than they were before. But many are still blindly impervious to the mounting spirit of revolt among land-starved tenants; they cannot see that through their intransigence they are digging their own graves.

Probably nothing could give a more powerful forward thrust to economic development, particularly in Latin

America, than to get a well-balanced program for equitable land use under way.

Instability of Governments

Another troublesome roadblock impeding the progress of our foreign aid program is the instability of governments in some of the host countries. Governments that frequently change are usually preoccupied with keeping themselves in power to the neglect of such long-range development as agriculture, education, and public works. An unstable government rarely has the prestige to establish an equitable tax system, one of the first essentials for economic growth.

The venal use of foreign aid materials by crafty politicians to secure favor with voters can test the patience and frustrate the efforts of the most competent AID men. No program can progress satisfactorily in a situation of political turmoil or irresponsible government.

Our traditional policy of dealing with the government in power, however unpopular it may be with its own citizens, lays us open to misinterpretation and mistrust. The villagers who see foreign aid materials consumed by the politician, the landlord, and the usurer, can hardly be expected to put their shoulders to the wheel with any enthusiasm.

However, in a situation as critical as that in which the world finds itself today, we can hardly always afford to sit back and await the millennium when governments will appear which are entirely to our liking. Moreover, among our electorate there appears to be less and less support for the idea of using aid as a club to persuade recalcitrant governments to line up on our side, or to keep raising the ante in a kind of international poker game with Communism.

But the achievements of foreign aid could be accelerated, if the United States were to be more firm in requiring the existence in the recipient country of a responsible government which has shown itself to be development minded.

Lack of Education

The inert weight of illiteracy which still hangs heavily over much of the world is a formidable bar to improvement in the life of millions. Estimates indicate that the developing countries are using only about one-tenth or less of their human potential.

Living as we do in a land where our youngsters are within easy reach of the improved school, it is hard for us to envision nations where only a small percentage of the children have any chance at an education at all, and where 90 per cent of the adult population is unable to read or write. Yet such conditions are common.

The most obvious problem brought about by a high illiteracy rate is the difficulty in disseminating information. How are the people to receive the instruction that they so badly need—improved health measures, child care, better farming, cooperatives—unless they can understand the new ideas? Radio and visual aids help, but in the long run these are not substitutes for the ability to read and write.

Widespread illiteracy also creates other problems less apparent, but bearing their social impact. The illiterate, feeling himself inferior and therefore insecure, is the more resistant to change. Unable to read, he may fall easy prey to the promises of demagogues.

A particular misfortune for the world is the high rate of illiteracy among women. There are still many communities where women are held in such low esteem that there seems little point in wasting time on their education.

More is at stake here than the individual's receptivity to new ideas and new skills. Only a literate populace can produce the leaders which an emerging society must have—the politicians, the professional men, the specialists, and the artisans. As Thomas Jefferson said: "A nation cannot be both untaught and free."

The situation in the Congo today should serve as a warning to other nations, demonstrating how lack of education can impede progress in the molding of government and other institutions. That country is one of the richest regions of the world in land, timber, and minerals; it is one of the poorest in human resources.

When the Congo came to statehood in June, 1960, only fourteen of its new leaders were college graduates. Because of this handicap, progress to date has been slow and erratic, and no one can tell what the future will be.

Other new nations suffer from this same problem, although to a less spectacular degree. If this condition is to be remedied, foreign aid must continue to give, as it is already giving, high priority to the improvement of literacy and the widespread development of at least elementary education.

Lack of Capital and Investment Appeal

In most developing nations, capital, next to land, is the missing key as far as physical resources are concerned. Crop yields are low, because neither tenants nor owners can get credit on reasonable terms to buy the needed seed, implements, and fertilizer. Indebtedness is high. Small owners mortgage their land. Laborers and tenants can only mortgage their services.

We in the West who are protected by law from usurious practices are inclined to regard the extortion of the moneylender as altogether reprehensible; yet there is something to be said in behalf of moneylenders.

Peasant farming is a risky business. In the face of such inexorable scourges as flood, drought, or insect plagues, there is little the farmer can do to protect himself. Backward methods raise the odds. The moneylender will advance funds under conditions where no bank would think of doing so. Thus, he performs his sordid service to the community, taking a loss here and there, but trying to tip the scales in his own favor by charging his ruinous interest rate.

The peasant cannot lift himself by his bootstraps. He seldom finds he has any margin with which to make needed improvements or from which he can save for a rainy day.

The notion of investing for development has not yet become popular among the rich in these countries. Much of their wealth, apart from their landed estates, is tied up in luxuries which can be flaunted, such as expensive automobiles, race horses, airplanes, and jewelry. When governments begin to wobble, those with liquid assets are quick to whisk them out of the country and into banks in foreign countries for safekeeping.

Capital for pump priming is vital to development, for in most localities new enterprises can only be started from scratch. The first steps are usually costly in relation to the revenue that can be expected. To reclaim land is one thing; but simultaneously to build dams for irrigation, to build roads to reach markets, to provide electric power for industries is something else again. Forests can be planted, but years will go by before any income from their timber crop can be realized. New schools, roads, and health services all need capital, but they constitute a form of investment from which there can be no direct financial return.

In securing development capital, most countries face a threefold task: First, the great mass of people must be encouraged to save even the smallest sums from their income. This takes time, especially where there is a mood of despair. A purposeful and enlightened leadership is required to persuade people voluntarily to deny themselves food, clothing, and shelter today so that their children may have more tomorrow. Yet countries that have pursued this course in earnest have been heartened by the results.

Second, a sense of social responsibility must be generated among the rich so they will invest their funds for progress at home rather than squirreling it into banks outside their borders.

Third, funds must come from abroad. Even though the poor save their mite and the elite invest a part of their surplus, there will still not be enough capital to meet the demands of rapid growth. Private investors are moving into lands where governments are stable. Our government is encouraging this. At best, outside funds from U.S. AID or other agencies can supply only a small percentage of the capital required. But that small percentage, working as a pump primer, can serve a purpose out of all proportion to the sums involved.

Inadequate Markets and World Trade

"No country can grow economically today unless it has a chance to sell its products to an advantage in the world market." This conclusion was reached by those attending the recent United Nations Conference on World Trade, held at Geneva, in 1963. After months of deliberation, the Conference agreed that freer world markets for the developing countries are a first step toward solution. But the delegates helplessly said: "No world-wide attack on this problem seems possible at this time."

To assuage the feelings of those from the "have-not" nations, the following resolution was passed: That developed nations should:

1. Do their best not to raise tariffs against manufactured goods from developing countries.

2. Raise their level of economic aid to 1 per cent of each country's total income.

3. Offer guarantees against any sudden drop in price of raw materials.

Stung with disappointment over the benign resolution, one delegate from Asia cried out: "The rich nations for two centuries have profited at our expense. We have endowed you with our raw materials and our cheap labor. Therefore, we are poor."

During the centuries of colonialism, an inflexible world pattern took form which has largely limited exports from developing countries to raw materials—ores, lumber, tea, rubber, crude oils, fiber, and spices. The prices of these products in the world markets are low compared to manufactured ones. It takes a lot of raw cacao or jute fiber to pay for a steel lathe or a dynamo!

Moreover, synthetics are constantly displacing raw materials, causing some prices to fluctuate widely. Those who demand "trade not aid" have a valid point. However, developing countries must, like Japan and some others, make every possible effort to enter the world market with goods that can compete.

Commenting on the meager results of the Geneva Conference on World Trade, the *Manchester Guardian* noted: "Each developed nation must accept a fair quota of manufactured goods. At present, aid is offset by falling raw commodity prices. The undernourished half of the world is a problem we cannot learn to live with, even if we wanted to."

If the rest of the world is slow to respond to foreign aid, one reason could be that the whole idea is not widely understood. The concept of one country assisting another gratuitously in normal times is still new.

The responsibilities of the recipient country are even less clearly understood. Many expect results to be dramatic, as the overnight blossoming of a desert, or some miracle that will bring a sudden end to unemployment. As John Kenneth Galbraith emphasized: "We, as well as recipient countries, lack a clear, purposeful view of what development involves." *

Near the close of World War II, a group of settlers from the hinterland of Australia called on the late John Curtin, Prime Minister, to complain because their progress was so slow and their lives so filled with hardship.

The Prime Minister stood beside the youngest of the group and placed a hand on his shoulder. "Son," he said, "when this country was being settled, the first generation broke their backs. The second generation broke their hearts. And the third generation entered into the promised land." Similarly, *our* viewpoint must be in terms of generations.

Although the handicaps to progress are clear enough, the rate at which foreign aid should be moving is difficult to determine. What shall we use as a yardstick? Are the poor getting more food, or better raiment and shelter? If we apply these tests alone, the answer is not satisfying.

But we err if we try to measure progress by dollar standards alone. A $25 increase in per capita income would make little sense to a Westerner if he could only use it to add

* "A Positive Approach to Foreign Aid," *Foreign Affairs Quarterly*, April, 1961, p. 445.

excess body weight or to buy an extra golf club. But for a peasant family, it could avert starvation, put a roof on the house, or maintain a child in school.

If we view the new developments for credit, irrigation, marketing, or the manufacture of fertilizers, the picture is much brighter.

Or, if we consider the intangibles, there is reason for real, if restrained, optimism. Among the encouraging signs which foreign aid workers see are changes in attitude, governments becoming development minded, capable technicians in some countries growing in number.

The journey to a better world is proving to be longer and steeper than we had hoped it would be. But the challenge to share the blessings of science with more than half of mankind appeals to what is deepest in the heart of America. No matter how steep or rocky the road, we dare not falter.

7

HOW MUCH IS OUR SHARE?

It surprises many people to learn that foreign aid is not peculiarly an American enterprise, that Uncle Sam is not alone as a faithful Atlas, carrying the world on his shoulders.

In a community meeting I attended recently, several people thought foreign aid payments were taking up one-third to one-half of the U.S. budget. The impression is easily accounted for. Most of the news stories on the subject of aid arise from Congressional debate over appropriations, which are usually attacked as too large.

Today, nearly every nation in the free world is giving aid to the underdeveloped countries. In 1963, their combined contribution came to $7.6 billion. Of this amount, the United States contributed 54 per cent. About half of what we gave, however, was designated for military purposes. Our total contribution added up to four and a half cents out of each government spending dollar for the year; currently, it is much less.

Moreover, the "rich uncle" myth loses even more of its substance when we realize that many of the countries being helped are drawing on their own resources to the limit before they seek assistance.

India, for the Third Five-Year Plan, is seeking only 16 per cent of the needed funds from outside her borders. Not only are her people taxing themselves to the utmost, but they are contributing labor and materials to an extent no one would have believed possible a few years ago. Our participation, though relatively small, may be viewed as that vital push that gets a project over the hill.

A mutual undertaking of countries hitherto remote can be a rewarding experience. Various examples are cited below.

In 1952, I was in New Delhi when two Norwegians arrived. Although the Prime Minister and a few ranking officials were at Palam Airport to receive them, their visit was virtually unpublicized. Late that afternoon, there was an official reception. In a simple ceremony, the two men announced that they had come as representatives of their government, and handed the treasurer of the Indian Commonwealth a check for 100,000 kroner ($20,000). That was Norway's first grant-in-aid. No strings were attached. During the conversation, however, it was learned that "certain segments of the Norwegian people had declared that they would be pleased to join in a project that could bring about an increased return for the Indian fisherman." The next morning, the two men, their announcement, and their gift made headlines in India's newspapers.

From that modest gift has grown the present Indo-Norwegian Project to improve India's fishing industry in its various aspects, from the deep sea nets to motorized boats, refrigeration, markets, public health, and education for the fishermen and their families.

In that same year, our Point Four program was just getting under way. Norway, as well as the rest of Western Europe, was still struggling to recover from the ravages of the war. In looking back after ten years to that first grant to India, Natvig Pederson, now Chairman of Norway's Foreign Aid Board, declared:

> We then called it an adventure. What else could it have been? We said to ourselves: "What on earth can Norway do in the midst of her own financial problems? Why should we try?" After five years of war and occupation, we were embarked on the tremendous task of rebuilding life in our own country. But we soon found we could proceed at an astonishing speed, thanks to aid through the Marshall Plan. I think the idea of aid to India sprang from a feeling of obligation to those who had not received such effective aid, also from a feeling of obligation to our own youth, and to our own future.

In 1962, Dean Rusk announced: "It is our policy to bring about the association of more of the democracies of Western Europe, North America, and Asia in promoting the prosperity of the free world."

But long before that time, Great Britain, Canada, France, and West Germany were already giving substantial aid. Even before the close of the war, Britain and France were extending aid to their colonies. The deprived world had not just one country helping, as many had assumed, but a dozen. In 1955, total aid given by all free countries except the U.S. came to $1.2 billion; these contributions have increased steadily.

In 1961, Belgium, Canada, Denmark, France, West Germany, Italy, Japan, the Netherlands, Norway, Portugal, and the United Kingdom gave a total of $2.4 billion. The largest contribution—$858 million—was given by France. Japan, a newcomer, gave $203 million; England gave $403 million; and West Germany, $289 million.

More than 90 per cent of France's assistance is in the form of grants. The Netherlands gave $60 million, in 1963. Of this amount, 94 per cent was in grants, and 6 per cent in loans which can be repaid in the currency of the recipient country.

Dr. Jan Hendrik Lubbers, of the Netherlands Mission to the United Nations, explained: "We attach no strings to either grants or loans, but we must study the capacity of a country to use the funds. At present we are giving .75 per cent of our gross national income. We plan to increase this to 1 per cent." *

France, in giving nearly 1.5 per cent of her total income for aid is spending a larger amount per capita than any of the other free countries. However, it must be recognized that much of this goes to her former colonies. Norway and Sweden have just joined the Netherlands in plans to commit 1 per cent of their gross national product to foreign aid.

We speak of Puerto Rico, an area struggling to rise by its own strength, as Operation Bootstrap. We would not normally think of a country so situated as a contributor of aid. But in 1962, Puerto Rico spent over $400,000 for the training expenses of nearly 5,000 students and observers sent there from other countries. Nor do we often think of countries down under as particularly concerned with the welfare of other nations. But Australia, under the Colombo Plan, has given grants of over $100 million, and training to nearly 3,000 technicians.

Spokesmen in the United States have maintained, from time to time, that the amounts of aid given by other free nations are not enough. The table below shows the total amount of U.S. aid compared with that given by other free countries for the years 1956 through 1962.

Amount of Economic Aid Given
(In Billions of Dollars)

	1956	1957	1958	1959	1960	1961	1962
United States	$2.0	$2.1	$2.4	$2.4	$2.8	$3.4	$2.6
Other free countries	1.2	1.7	2.0	2.1	2.1	2.5	2.5

SOURCE: Agency for International Development, 1963 Report.

The figures show a steady rise in the contributions of other countries. This is particularly significant since the

* An address before the New York Branch of the Society for International Development, December, 1963.

money is nearly all given as economic assistance. A considerable portion is in the form of grants.

Another question often asked concerns the ability of a country to provide aid and the percentage of the gross national product given in this way. The following table again compares the U.S. with other countries.

Aid as a Percentage of the Gross National Product

	1956	1957	1958	1959	1960	1961	1962	1963
Other free countries	.49	.63	.70	.68	.62	.71	.72	.74
United States	.48	.47	.55	.50	.56	.66	.70	.56

SOURCE: Agency for International Development, 1964 Report.

The figures show that at present other free nations are appropriating a larger percentage of their national product than we are. We must also bear in mind that a considerable part of our allotment is in the form of military aid.

Contrary to general opinion, our burden has eased considerably. As a percentage of the total national product, it has dropped from 2 per cent in the first months of the Marshall Plan to .52 per cent at present.

Since 1956, the Soviet Union has been using aid as an instrument of its foreign policy. The pledges of the Sino-Soviet bloc announced since that time totaled $7.1 billion by 1964. However, it is reported that only a small part of the promised aid was delivered. David E. Bell has estimated that economic aid extended by all Communist nations totaled $1.3 billion in 1964.

The Communist bloc reports that in 1964 it had approximately 10,000 technical workers engaged in various aid functions overseas. The number for all other countries is estimated at 50,000.*

Soviet aid is offered largely in the form of loans and mili-

* Many of these, like those of Russia and China, are skilled mechanics. Comparatively few are technical specialists.

tary equipment. Only 4 per cent of the total is accounted for by grants. The interest rate reported is ordinarily 2.5 per cent, although there are instances of interest-free loans. Presumably because they have less capital, the satellite countries charge interest, ranging from 2.5 up to 5 per cent.

It is easy for us to assume that ours is the only nation to suffer disappointments. Since the U.S.S.R. entered the field, it too has encountered most of the problems that have plagued us, besides some that are uniquely its own. Their first technicians, like too many of our own, were strangers who could not speak the language. Their machines were not always well adapted; the tractors which they supplied did not prove popular. However, it is rather widely agreed that Russian technicians adapt readily and more freely among the common people.

Aid by International Agencies

No discussion of our future aid responsibilities would be complete without reference to the work done by international agencies and nongovernmental groups such as foundations and churches.

From time to time, observers express the opinion that our aid programs—or at least more of their functions—could well be turned over to international agencies. For this reason, we ought to have an idea who these agencies are and what they are doing. Of these, the United Nations Special Fund in cooperation with the U.N. "family of agencies" is probably best known. Among these cooperating agencies are:

World Health Organization
Food and Agriculture Organization
United Nations Educational, Scientific and Cultural Organization
International Labor Organization
United Nations International Children's Emergency Fund

The United States, through AID, takes an active part in the far-flung enterprises of the U.N. Special Fund. Our contributions to this phase of its activities have amounted to approximately 40 per cent of the agency's annual budget for social and economic development.

Why shouldn't the U.S. channel all or at least the larger part of its foreign aid through the U.N.? Could not a world-wide international agency, acting multilaterally, function with greater impact than an agency of a single country? Could not such an agency deal more objectively with the stubborn problems of development, and at a lower cost? Certain development problems are indeed international in character, as witness the case of locusts.

An international body enjoys an advantage when it comes to the control of livestock diseases such as rinderpest. Attacking the mosquito or the tsetse fly or the locust plague often calls for concerted action across national borders, as does the development of some river valleys such as the Sutlej between India and Pakistan, or the Mekong of Southeast Asia.

In nations recently freed from colonial rule, the spirit of national pride runs high. Their eagerness to flex their muscles, to seek world recognition is understandable. To them, agencies such as those of the United Nations appear as appealing ventures in a new kind of partnership. These nations would, with less hesitation, turn to an international authority rather than to a single country.

Surveys and studies are often necessary before a decision can be reached on a major project such as a power dam, or before a loan can be advanced for whatever purpose. These are called feasibility studies. Where only two countries are involved, it is harder to be objective. Impersonal recommendations of an international task force are much more likely to be acceptable.

The U.N. can draw its technical personnel from a wider area than can any one country. Asians point out that where technicians from their own part of the world are employed, they are already informed as to the culture and terrain. The cost of a project is thus less than when Western personnel has to be moved in, involving higher salaries, moving costs, and housing in the field.

In 1963, the FAO and other agencies executing projects in behalf of the U.N. Special Fund had a combined staff of approximately 1,575 technical experts. They were recruited from 55 member countries. The Special Fund operating budget of $72.4 million represented contributions from 112 member nations.

World-wide support for the U.N. Special Fund has grown steadily, increasing from $25 million to $72.4 million in 1963. Of the latter amount, the United States contributed $30 million. This is expected to be increased—provided it does not exceed 40 per cent of the total contributions of all countries. Our Congress has set up this restriction as an incentive for other nations to increase their contributions, with the objective of making the U.N. program more truly a representative international endeavor. Within the last two years, all member nations were asked to increase their contributions to the enlarged program that is financed by the U.N. Special Fund.

But the United States' participation with the U.N. goes far beyond the mere allocation of funds. The paths of U.S. and U.N. technicians meet often as they join forces on many projects.

After all has been said, a multilateral agency faces many of the same problems encountered by a unilateral assistance program. The U.N. has to operate over a broad and varied front; coordination is difficult. A loosely knit, heterogeneous body cannot always allocate its development funds fairly on the basis of need. Lobbying and pressures arise. Personnel and resources must sometimes be spread out too thin to be effective. Supervision becomes difficult. Some U.N. members are able to make only token grants.

However, as the number of successful projects multiplies and as our country gains further experience in international cooperation, we may expect that all nations will choose to make far greater use of this multilateral partnership for economic growth.

Nations working in concord can and will accomplish more than nations working unilaterally. With the food situation becoming so acute, the need for a unified world-wide plan of attack is urgent. For such leadership, we must look more and more to the U.N. Special Fund and the Food and Agricultural Organization.

The Colombo Plan

Another international authority, the Colombo Plan—in which the U.S. is also a participant—deserves to be better understood. Like the U.N. it is closely interrelated with our aid efforts in much of Asia.

The Colombo Plan, like our Point Four, came into being after the close of World War II. Much of Southeast Asia was in a state similar to devastated Europe when it prompted the Marshall Plan. Factories and harbors had been destroyed; shipping, railroads, and other forms of transportation were disrupted. Population had increased during the war years with no corresponding increase in food.

The young men who had been to war caught a glimpse of the abundance that technology can provide. Returning home, these veterans became impatient nationalists; they demanded immediate reforms. Communists circulated freely in the cities; the hills and villages had their guerrilla bands. The age-old yoke of hunger, poverty, and disease bore down on the backs of the masses with a weight that was even more painful than before.

These were some of the threats that hung over the foreign ministers of the British Commonwealth countries when they met in Colombo, Ceylon, on January 9, 1950. India, Pakistan, and Burma had just been given their freedom; other countries were demanding theirs. The ministers tried to concentrate on political matters, but gnawing poverty and economic blight always came to the fore as the overriding issues.

It was during one of these sobering sessions that the idea for the Colombo Plan was born, representing a joint effort of the Commonwealth countries to solve their economic dilemma.

The original members were Australia, Great Britain and

her territories of Malaya and Borneo, Canada, Ceylon, India, New Zealand, and Pakistan. A consultative committee was set up which later designed the Technical Cooperation Scheme. The Plan now includes all the countries of South and East Asia, as well as Australia, Canada, the United Kingdom, New Zealand, and the United States. The United Nations agencies help out with personnel and grants. (The U.S. joined in 1959.)

The Colombo Plan embodies several unusual features. First, it is founded on the principle of mutual assistance. Member countries are "joined in covenant to aid each other as equals." The industrialized nations contribute a lion's share of the funds, but all members are expected to give as much as they can. This stipulation softens the distinction between donor and recipient countries.

A second feature places the relationships among the twenty-two countries on a bilateral, or country-to-country, basis. The over-all Consultative Committee meets annually, and there is a small continuing staff council in Colombo. But the organization serves largely as an umbrella under which Commonwealth countries can work bilaterally. It is believed that this arrangement not only speeds up the program but reduces overhead expense.

The fiscal year 1962–63 saw 936 Colombo Plan experts at work in the member nations; their classification by country of origin was: Australia, 68; Britain, 59; Canada, 40; Malaya Federation, 67; India, 111; Japan, 67; New Zealand, 24; United States, 499; Vietnam, 1. Education, including technical training, accounted for 25 per cent of the experts; agriculture, public health, and engineering, 15 per cent each. Ten per cent were engaged in banking; the others were distributed among fisheries, social services, printing, etc.

U.S. AID has development projects of various kinds under way with all member countries of the Colombo Plan. Limited amounts of materials and equipment are provided, the idea being to get on with the job as rapidly as possible.

The Plan is not without its weaknesses. Some say it is too loosely supervised—that it lacks coordination. An AID mission director in South Asia said he finds the Plan too small, its resources spread too thinly. Others complain that it lacks the centralized authority needed for effective administration. "Without an administrative head, it only marks time," they say.

If we make a judgment on the basis of the increase in food production or the pitifully small increase in per capita income, the results appear insignificant. But success here, as with the United Nations, or our own foreign aid program, cannot be measured by the statistical yardstick alone. The Colombo Plan's White Paper, issued in October, 1963, speaks of an "augmented attitude of mutual trust among members . . . the groundwork for permanent development that has been laid . . . significant industrial growth . . . the inestimable amount of good will that has been generated —the great number of future workers trained."

In November, 1963, a member of the Consultative Council in Colombo was evaluating the past and looking to the future, and in substance he told me: "Achievements of the first decade are hardly dramatic. But at least a firm structure has been built. That is of paramount importance, as we can see now that we are joining with the U.N. in the decade of development. Certainly we have no reason for despair."

Non-Government Agencies

One of the characteristics of American life is the large number of private or non-governmental agencies engaged in service abroad. The 1965 Conference on International Development in Washington, D.C., was attended by delegates from 115 agencies, all of whom had operations overseas. Most Americans contribute to the work of one or more of these agencies. For the sake of clarity, they may be grouped in three classes:

1) Private agencies—foundations and business firms,

2) Voluntary agencies—churches and other groups which depend on voluntary contributions,

3) Service agencies—those whose main contribution is the work of volunteers.

The Ford Foundation functions today in sixteen countries. The Foundation's work abroad began in 1952, with grants to India totaling $3.5 million for the training of village workers, and for projects designed to increase food production. The work has since spread to other countries of South Asia, the Near East, and Latin America. It has been widened to include the humanities, the arts, engineering, agriculture, and public health. If there is a central thread running through this wide range of activities, it would be the development of people.

The Rockefeller Foundation, through its program of aid to research and teaching, carries on projects in 88 countries. Active outside the United States for nearly half a century, its practical efforts are focused mainly on public health and the improvement of crops and livestock. The Foundation offers a generous number of fellowships for advanced study in these and other fields. Its plant research has developed a new variety of corn adapted to areas with irregular rainfall. Normally, a corn crop is lost if there is no rain for a period of weeks, especially at earing time. This extraordinary variety is bred so that it becomes dormant in a period of drought, then resumes growth when rain comes.

At Los Baños, in the Philippines, the Ford and Rockefeller foundations are jointly supporting the International Rice Research Institute, the former providing $7.5 million to establish the Institute, and the latter supplying $500,000 a year for operating costs. The Institute, in cooperation with the Philippines and other rice-growing countries, is conducting tests on over 8,000 kinds of rice grown in various parts of the world. It would be hard to overstate the potential value of the IRRI to the peace and well-being of mankind.

The Near East Foundation has a long record of distinguished service in agricultural improvement, adult education, public health, and home economics, particularly in countries of the Near East. Our foreign aid program in those lands received much help from workers already trained under this Foundation.

The contributions of many other foundations and of business firms are also significant.

Voluntary Agencies

It is often said that no army can withstand the force of an idea whose time has come. The idea of nations helping each other with the exchange of technical aid has long been growing. The record extends back for more than a century and a half. William Carey was the groundbreaker, in 1794. A clergyman, scholar, and agriculturist, he had gone to work in India under the auspices of an English church. In that year, Carey had a moment of inspiration. He wrote to his brother in England: "Send me yearly the best seeds and tubers. Send also sickles and plowshares. This is a good farming country, but the peoples' comforts are so few, and their food so meager. Many starve."

In those days, travel to India was by sailing vessel, a voyage of perhaps a year or more around the Cape of Good Hope. But Carey's brother answered his plea. The clergyman's garden plots near Calcutta became famous for their improved varieties of fruits, vegetables, and cereal grains. Carey had no budget for this work, but he distributed seeds and cuttings as widely as possible. By 1830, he had helped to found the Agri-horticultural Society of India. At that time, the only other such societies extant were in Italy and Scotland. During the century that followed, church workers in other parts of the world were beginning to take an interest in agriculture and in the economic well-being of the people.

In 1876, W. O. Clark, of Massachusetts, then lecturing in Japan on Christian ethics, helped to establish the Imperial Agricultural College at Sapporo. In the decade from 1897 on, the work of the churches in agriculture began to take still more definite form.

William Bell, a graduate in agriculture from Cornell University, was sent to Africa to assist local farmers in improving their crops. J. B. Knight, a manual arts expert, was assigned to India to help in developing cottage industries—spinning, weaving, sheet metal, and shoemaking. In 1902, Henry House, a minister, established the American Farm School at Salonia, Greece. At the same time, Benjamin H.

Hunnicutt founded the Lavras Agricultural College in Brazil. Other pioneer agricultural colleges were opened in China, India, Turkey, Egypt, Lebanon, and Chile.

George Roberts, commissioned to East Africa in 1907, chose to work exclusively among farmers. He was still there in 1957, when he showed me a thriving crop of hybrid corn in his neighbor's field. "That field is the place where Mulba Joseph, then a farmer, and I introduced the first moldboard plow ever to be seen in this area," he said. "That was in 1912. Today there are thousands of such plows in use. The hoe and the pointed stick have been discarded in favor of plows and other improved implements."

These unobtrusive efforts were warmly welcomed by most of the people, although there was more resistance to change in those early years than aid workers encounter today.

National leaders were soon playing a prominent part in economic development. In Japan, Toyohiko Kagawa became the devoted "servant of the poor" as he helped to establish cooperative societies. Japanese tell us that modern agriculture owes much to Kagawa, whose early work was most helpful in laying the foundation on which present successful cooperatives have been built.

During the early 1930's, K. T. Paul, son of an Indian bishop, became the pioneer of the rural reconstruction movement. Seeing the farmers' need for credit on fair terms, Paul once cried out: "How in conscience can an agrarian country rise when its farmers are half-starved and chained by usury!"

In 1964, there were 360 American agriculturists assigned and supported by churches for work in 48 countries.

Some church denominations have departments of their own, especially for relief and rehabilitation. Of these, the American Friends Service Committee is one of the oldest and best known. Founded at Oxford, England, in 1652, the Religious Society of Friends quickly turned early to "healing and philanthropy as robust alternatives to war."

"This effort," said William Penn, "does not suggest withdrawal from ordinary life. Rather, it strives to enable men to live better within it, and excites their endeavors to mend it."

Most of the work abroad is carried on by mature college students who serve on a voluntary basis. In commenting on the kind of young people they send, Amos Peasley said: "We seek sensitive spirits of divine ordinariness. Building the institutions of peace is the greatest enterprise of our time. We must build and rebuild and then, mayhap, must build again."

Catholic Relief Service of the National Catholic Welfare Conference is the Church's overseas agency for distributing food, medicine, and clothing, and assisting in other phases of community development. The agency works closely with the United States Government's Food for Peace Program.

In Latin America especially, the Catholic Church is doing outstanding work, through cooperative credit societies, as well as in other ways.

Church World Service, founded in 1946, is the over-all overseas relief agency for thirty-four American Protestant denominations. Established at the close of World War II, CWS gave special attention to assisting political refugees, helping to heal the gaping wounds left in the wake of war, and has continued various other relief and rehabilitation services.

A characteristic of CWS is its quick response to emergencies. For example, when Iran suffered an earthquake two years ago, CWS had two planeloads of food and medicine in the air within twenty-four hours. The CWS rehabilitation program includes anything from the supply of seeds, farm implements, and tools for craftsmen to medicines and help with supplies for building homes.

The settlement of thousands of refugees has been a unique contribution of church service agencies. To cite one example, in April, 1964, these agencies, operating jointly, saw No. 15,200 in a stream of Cuban refugees safely relocated in the United States.

Special Services

For the past eleven years, International Voluntary Service has sent young people to villages and towns in the Near East and Asia to "form links of friendship and help by means of projects large and small."

The people of neglected areas appreciate schools, relief supplies, and literacy classes. But what warms their hearts above all else is the presence of those who come to live and work with them. The IVS sends out carefully chosen young people to do just this. They have no program to promote or material goods to distribute. Their only assets are good will and whatever they can do as teachers, laborers, or technical helpers in the many aspects of village improvement.

IVS, supported largely by the "peace churches"—that is, the Friends, Brethren, and Mennonites—appoints the young people for two-year terms and provides maintenance and a few dollars a month for pocket money. U.S. AID makes grants to IVS for the support of projects in agriculture, education, public health, and various other facets of human development.

These young Americans, although few in number, have been so successful and respected that they had a great influence on the later development of the Peace Corps. Two attractive aspects of this effort are the quality of work done and the low cost. The average annual cost of maintaining a worker in the field is just under $5,000, including all his expenses abroad as well as headquarter costs in the United States. In 1964, IVS had about 200 volunteers on assignment in 11 countries.

Although the Peace Corps is government-supported, its members also serve in a voluntary way and on a subsistence basis. They enjoy no diplomatic immunity and receive neither hardship nor cost-of-living allowances. Like the IVS men and women, they live and work among the people. While most of them are in their twenties, a few are over sixty. Teaching accounts for the largest number; agriculture comes next, with calls for workers in youth clubs, village health, cooperatives, and handicrafts as well.

Peace Corps service is viewed by many young people as a two-way street. A young woman, recently returned from two years in Thailand, voiced the sentiments of many Peace Corps volunteers when she told me: "All those with whom I've worked have been so kind and friendly. They have taught me so much more than I could teach them. We all cried a little when time came for me to leave. I hope I can go back again soon."

In welcoming a group of young men to Nigeria, the Prime Minister declared: "I am sure your coming to Nigeria will be mutually helpful to us and to you."

Many consider experience with the Peace Corps as a proving ground for later service with AID or the diplomatic corps. Such training in itself could repay much of what we are spending. The Peace Corps idea has proved so attractive that twenty-six other nations are now at work on plans for their own counterpart organizations.

Less known but equally important is the British organization, Volunteers for Service Overseas. This is an independent agency formed in 1958 "to allow young people to spend a year or more in service abroad." Applicants, usually between the ages of eighteen and twenty-seven, are drawn from industry as well as from universities. Here, too, the greatest demand is for teachers.

The VSO headquarters in London pays travel expenses only. It is supported by contributions received from churches, individuals, and business firms. Unlike the Peace Corpsmen, the volunteers are provided room and board overseas by the school, farm, or other agency abroad for which they work. One advantage of this procedure is that the arrival of volunteers is anticipated and they are given specific job assignments. According to the volunteers' handbook: "An allowance may also be given by the sponsor overseas to help to replace shoes and clothes. But this is not to be expected."

Recruits must meet high standards of education, technical skill, and character. Instructions to volunteers suggest that "applicants display a mood of humility, since you will often gain much more than you can give." Currently there are 790 volunteers under VSO serving in 36 countries.

The above are but a few samples of the varied array of nongovernmental forces that are giving a hand to economic development. Their number reflects the deep interest of our people. Although most of them are handicapped by insufficient funds, this lack is compensated for, in part, by other advantages.

The first is a constancy of effort. Young people who serve under the churches as missionaries generally choose overseas work as a career. Their work is not affected by political change or the limitations of temporary assignment. The long-term approach allows workers the opportunity to attack the causes of poverty as well as to relieve its symptoms.

The ever-present financial stringency compels them to work in the least expensive way and to avoid waste, factors too easily overlooked in governmental operations. By their concentration on the quality of work and the advancement of human relations, they help to create a climate in which governments can work more fruitfully. An AID field man in the Near East said that 60 per cent of the national leaders whom they employed had been trained in schools and colleges sponsored by churches and other private groups.

While private groups make an invaluable contribution, we must remember that they are extremely limited by lack of funds and the small number of technically qualified persons. The major tasks of development will always have to be borne by governments with their immense resources.

How Much Should We Share with Other Nations?

How large a bite is foreign aid currently taking from our national income? The Eighty-eighth Congress voted $3.2 billion for the year 1964–65. This represents .53 per cent of our gross national product. Around three cents out of each dollar the government spends will go for aid. Two cents per dollar will actually go for economic aid, or .3 per cent of our gross national product.

Mindful of the drastic cuts made by Congress in 1963, President Johnson tried to avoid trouble for the 1964–65 budget by presenting a preshrunk request for $3.5 billion. *The New York Times* called this a "bare bones budget, below what is needed to get our share of the job done."

Senator Jacob Javits observed that if we reduce our aid, others will find occasion to do the same.

In defending the 1964–65 request to Congress, Secretary of State Dean Rusk explained: "This is just one-fifteenth of what we spend on military preparedness."

Some still think of foreign aid as charity: "The rich should give to the poor," it is said. Barbara Ward advises us against taking this view. "All are developing countries, but the rate of growth is so uneven that we are heading toward chaos. Aid must be sufficient to assure more balanced growth for all."

Holland's world scholar, M. J. L. Dols, summarized the findings of the World Food Congress held in Amsterdam in September, 1962, as follows: "Funds for economic aid can no longer be viewed as charity, but our bounden duty to this period of history. Those who speak of our spending the next fifty to eighty years at the job may be more realistic than the year-to-year planners."

Time is running out. The idea of democracy is new in most developing countries. Its roots are still near the surface. People pleading for jobs, schools, food, and shelter will not wait indefinitely. Some leaders in developing nations are fearful lest they be forced to sacrifice their newly found democracy in order to get some of the things their people are calling for.

What would be a fair amount for us to pay? With only 7 per cent of the world's population, we enjoy more than 40 per cent of the world's income. Our aid burden has declined over the years, while our gross national product mounts. We gave 2 per cent of our gross product at the beginning of the Marshall Plan, in 1949. We are giving .5 per cent of it today. As a share of the federal budget, foreign aid has declined from 11 per cent in 1949 to 3 per cent in 1965.

According to the U.S. Department of Commerce, we Americans spent the following in the fiscal year 1962–63: *

Luxuries	*Billions*
Cosmetics	$2.5
Toilet articles and preparations	3.3
Toys and sports supplies	5.2
Malt and distilled liquors	7.8
Tobacco products	8.0

Commenting on the above in *Newsweek,* William Hard reflected: "We could cut down on our luxuries by 10 per cent, double our expenditures on foreign aid, and perhaps be as well off."

Before me is a letter from the president of a national farm organization. He writes: "I am convinced that most people in the United States are very much in favor of *economic aid and Food for Peace.* But they demand that it reach the people and deal directly with poverty. We are at present only marking time. This is dangerous."

There was a sense of excitement when the late President Kennedy announced plans for dispatching men to the moon. The fact that it would cost us as much as we are paying out for aid over a ten-year period received slight attention. I do not suggest that we give up the moon idea, but a far more urgent challenge awaits us here on earth. If we fail in this, it would make little difference whether we ever reach the moon.

It is hard to suggest a specific amount that we should continue to give. But many of our people are dissatisfied with our meager and erring effort. Americans who favor a stronger aid program are not prodigals. Rather, they want what Walter Bagehot long ago called "vigorous moderation." We must rise above our inclination to think only in minimum terms in this respect. Our people will respond

* *Survey of Current Business,* U.S. Department of Commerce, July, 1963.

again as they have in the past whenever they are challenged to a great task that is intelligently and efficiently administered.

Congress might do well to ask several of our most able statesmen and economists to make a study to determine our obligation over the next ten years.

Larger contributions will be required from all advanced nations as more efficient methods of working are developed and as the poor countries advance to a point where they can profitably use larger amounts of outside capital.

Our responsibilities abroad must, of course, be considered in the light of practical considerations at home. Our own economy must be kept strong. We have our own balance of payments problem, unemployment, and areas of poverty to consider.

But in the long run a studied and well-administered foreign aid program could help in the solution of these problems. This seems to be the opinion of the European countries planning to give 1 per cent or more of their gross national product.

The administrator of AID, David E. Bell, and his associates, have tightened up the organization, sharpened its objectives, and are striving for further improvements. As soon as we have a program that can operate with *economy and all reasonable precision,* we should begin using at least 1 per cent of our gross national income for aid and anticipate a larger amount during the years ahead. One per cent of our gross national product would be $6 billion, one-half of the percentage we gave in 1952 when our gross national product was but one-third of what it now is.

At present, this would include both military and economic aid. If, as noted in Chapter 9, the military component can be separated from the foreign aid budget, that would effect the amount to be appropriated for purely economic aid.

From the standpoint of political security, we are spending $5.25 per person per week on military defense, to buy time, and keep the peace. We are spending $.35 per person per week to lay the actual social and economic foundations of enduring peace. These figures are clearly out of proportion.

What kind of a foreign aid program would be worth a larger appropriation? In warfare, very little consideration is given to economy in the use of funds or material; in foreign aid, success is contingent upon the prudent use of all resources.

Thus far, we have outlined the course of foreign aid from its beginning up to the present time. From here on, we will consider some needed changes and improvements, for it is not possible to achieve genuine economic growth, let alone political and social development, without major refinements in our approach. In making these suggestions, I shall lean heavily upon facts gathered from consultations with scores of aid specialists in the United States and overseas.

The suggestions are offered with the hope that they will stimulate study and dialogue on the part of the planners and the general public. This could lead to improvements that are essential if our aid is to regain public confidence and achieve its objectives.

8

THREE WEAK LINKS

OUR FOREIGN aid program is in need of repair at three crucial points: (1) we should focus directly upon those for whom it is intended; (2) we should utilize the power of women and the village homes; (3) we should give more adequate support to basic education.

I present these points largely in terms of rural situations because the problems of developing countries are so largely those of the rural people. Their needs are often the most difficult and the most inadequately met. Although we find tragic conditions of poverty in the cities, much of this is among those who fled there to escape the impossible degradation of the villages.

Help for Those at the Bottom of the Ladder

President Kennedy, in his inaugural address, made this pledge:

> To those peoples in the huts and villages of half the globe struggling to break the bonds of mass misery, we pledge our best efforts to help them help themselves, for whatever period

> is required—not because the Communists may be doing it, not because we seek their votes, but because it is right. If a free society cannot help the many who are poor, it cannot save the few who are rich.

Thus, he cogently stated the necessity for helping those at the bottom of the economic ladder.

Who are these people who cling precariously to the lowest rung? Naturally their individual characteristics vary from one country to another. But there is a surprising similarity in their situations. They make up anywhere from 30 to 50 per cent of the population of developing countries. They break down generally into four main groups, although there is some overlapping.

By far the largest group consists of the landless laborers who live in little huts off to one side of the fields. These are the people who provide the labor. They do the planting, weed the crops, and carry in the harvest. For the remainder of the year they are often idle, except when labor is needed for work on roads, schools, or other public works.

Famine and epidemic strike them first; the benefits of education, public health, and medical care reach them last. They are also among the fastest growing in numbers.

The next largest group is what the professional agronomists know as the sub-subsistence farmers who expend their labors on soil so poor or fields so small that they cannot manage decently to feed their families. Some of their farms are remote and isolated; others are in regions where the soil has long been starved. In underdeveloped countries as a whole, between 70 and 90 per cent of these farmers are hopelessly in debt. In South and Southeast Asia, the figure averages about 80 per cent. Leon Florez, a rural banker, has estimated the figure for the Philippines to be as high as 90 per cent.

The slum dwellers come next, living on the periphery of the cities. As many as 3,000 families without visible means of support huddle in tents and shacks in the vicinity of

Calcutta's Sealdah Railway Station alone. One of the acute problems of our time is the growing number of these migrants who seek refuge in the larger cities on all the continents. Their moves are largely motivated by hope for a better life; when they are disillusioned, the results are pathetic.

Perhaps the smallest group numerically among the disenfranchised are the craftsmen; shoemakers, spinners, and weavers. But they are also the most rapidly increasing, for they are the ones being pushed from their livelihood by industry at the most rapid rate.

Countries remain underdeveloped because the latent abilities of these people remain underdeveloped. All in all, they constitute a force to be reckoned with, for they no longer are willing to accept their lot with resignation, as being inevitable. They see the skyscrapers and the luxury apartment houses going up. They walk barefoot to market along the superhighway that foreign aid has often helped to build, with no more ease than they did along the old dirt trail.

In an aid program that has as its objective the upgrading of the human condition, these unfortunates should be a prime target, for they are the miserable of the world.

If we are to consider the matter of sheer survival in terms of augmenting the food supply to keep pace with the growing population, their welfare is essential. For these are the producers. It is their arms, their experience, their hard work that grow the crops on the large plantations, on the haciendas.

If the battle against hunger is to be won, we must also enlist the help of the millions of peasant farmers. The food problem will not be solved basically by shipping food surpluses from the more fortunate countries to the less fortunate, however important this is.

Thus far, our efforts have largely missed the lives of those at the bottom of the ladder. There are so many of them and they are so poor that this becomes a monumental undertaking. We will tackle it successfully only if we focus our sights more sharply and if we are fully aware of the important stakes involved.

The developing nations' demand for heavy industries and the fondness for prestige projects such as airfields or spectacular new office buildings tend to blind us to the necessity of relieving the crucial deficiencies.

Besides, there are two schools of thought as to where a foreign aid program should begin. Some say it should begin with the larger and more efficient farmers at the top of the economic ladder. Those who hold this point of view argue that since the big farmers have the best land, greater skills, and more capital, they are the ones who can make the best use of technical aid. These farmers are literate; they are receptive to new ideas. If they are given help, they will produce more food, and all will prosper in the end.

In discussions with those who advance this point of view, one finds that they are inclined to dismiss the unhappy masses at the bottom of the ladder, the landless millions, the sub-subsistence farmers, as a welfare problem. It is doubtful whether any country on earth—developed or underdeveloped—can afford to carry such a welfare load. Nor can any developing country hope to rise economically or assure its freedom with such a large segment of its people trapped in a morass of poverty.

It is easy to assume that since these people now have little and are producing little, they will inevitably be replaced by farmers with greater resources and greater skills. We see this happening to a degree today in the United States. We reason that it must also happen elsewhere. We forget that in the United States we have an abundance of land, a high degree of mechanization, and opportunities for work in industry to absorb the surplus farm population. These conditions do not hold true for underdeveloped areas where land is scarce, population dense, and there are so few opportunities for employment in industry.

It is understandable that until now we have followed the easier road. Loans can be negotiated to build factories and buildings which will not only produce income, but represent a tangible result from our effort. But we can no longer afford to overlook the infinitely more difficult but absolutely essential task of improving the lot of the low man on the totem pole.

Many still maintain that the obstacles in the way of helping the landless or sub-subsistence farmer are too formidable to justify the effort, that these people are untutored, enmeshed in outmoded ways of doing things, unreceptive to change or improvement of any kind.

I must say that with a few exceptions this has not been my experience. I have worked in the fields with these very people over a period of many years. I have listened to them as they have described their aspirations, and I have been impressed by their moderation and reasonableness, as well as by the intensity of their yearning for a better life. I have seen with what frugality they use any financial help that is given, for they know how much toil and backache it takes to earn a dollar.

But some conventional economists still say it cannot be done; we cannot begin from the bottom. In answer to that assertion, we have the experience of Father Dan McClellan with the Quechua Indians of Peru, as related to me by Father Robert Kearns of the Maryknoll Fathers, while I was in Peru:

"High on the 11,500-foot plateau by Lake Titicaca, the patience of the peons had run out," he said. "Without land or decent food, the Communist gospel appealed to them. Something had to be done.

"Our credit union man is Dan McClellan, Father Dan they call him. But I've been close to that work for over twenty years." Vigorous and confident, Father Kearns chose his words with precision.

"Father Dan decided that what the people needed was a 'poor man's bank.'

"Back in 1953, when we started the first credit union, most people advised against it. Sociologists, businessmen, and government officers said it wouldn't work. They said

'The Indians have no security; no experience. They'll only take the money and get drunk.'

"We agreed that Puno was perhaps the most unlikely place on earth to open a credit union. The Indians were mostly illiterate, desperately poor. Their small patches of land were arid and rocky.

"But Father Dan believed in people. He knew very little about credit unions or banking, so he read all the books and reports he could get. Whenever he heard of a cooperative somewhere that failed, he hustled off to find out the reasons. Finally, he said, 'These people must have money to work for them, working money. Paying 60 per cent interest, they're servants of money, not its masters.'

"In 1955, Father Dan met with twenty-three Indians who were willing to become charter members of the first credit union. The best they could do was to scrape up 750 soles, the equivalent of $28, for operating capital.

"Things began to happen. Most Indians hoard a little money as protection in case of death or other emergency. When they saw they could trust their little 'bank' and that they could deposit their money and get interest, money began coming up from holes in the dirt floors, from chinks in the wall, and from cornhusk mattresses."

"What do the borrowers do with the money?" I asked.

"Loans are made from 28 soles ($1.00) up. Members buy seeds, fertilizers, improved chickens, help to build and equip schools, send children away to school, pay for land, build better houses."

"But how can you loan where there is no chattel for security?" I questioned.

"True, the people do not have chattel as security, but they have something better; they have integrity and pride in their cooperative society. Although half the members are illiterate, they are not ignorant. We have practically no losses from default in payments. Family pride prevents that. If one can't make his payments on time, family members will step in and do it.

"Local businessmen, government workers, and farmers of

means were willing to join and deposit funds as soon as they were sure the funds would be safe.

"Today, after nine years, that first credit union has 3,200 members. The members have saved and earned around $350,000."

I learned that from the first society of 23 members in 1953, the people have developed 270 credit unions with a combined membership of over 60,000. Total savings of members comes to over $2 million. Father McClellan's plan has since been put into effect in many other places in Latin America.

What Father Kearns told me was confirmed by Earl Smith, AID's agriculturist for the area. He said: "That whole part of southern Peru might be in political chaos today were it not for the work of the Maryknoll Fathers and the credit unions. Communist agents had marked that district for easy takeover. The Indians were in ferment. But now many of the agents themselves have gone over and are working for the credit union movement. The credit union members have learned how to work with the little they have and lick their own problems. That explains the atmosphere of self-confidence, the spirit of pride you find there."

Let us take another situation. While traveling in central India in 1953, I came to a small village where the main occupation was weaving.

If one were to have taken that village as typical, he would have held little hope for the future of the nation. The weavers were growing old; their old-fashioned handlooms were in a state of decay. The quality of cloth they turned out was so poor that there was little market for it. Since they produced almost nothing, they could buy almost nothing.

The plight of the village caught the interest of an Indian businessman. As an experiment, he underwrote the purchase of twenty up-to-date, improved handlooms. With this incentive, the younger people in the village were now eager to learn the weaver's craft.

The government stepped in and a weavers' cooperative was formed to buy yarn and market cloth. On the day of my visit, ten years later, more than 3,000 improved hand-looms were clacking away. A new generation of weavers was supporting its families by the production of marketable cloth.

The road to town fifteen miles away had been improved. Five buses were operating. Two small factories had been opened. Farmers, carpenters, potters, and tailors were more prosperous because the weavers could buy what they produced.

We cannot expect healthy economic growth if we leave out those at the bottom of the ladder. How can we build industries in cities when nearly half the people are outside the money economy with no means for buying the bicycles, clocks, plows, and shoes that are produced?

Industry in an underdeveloped country can prosper only as the great submerged sector of the people has means to buy what is manufactured.

Of course, a certain amount of aid to factories and larger farms does seep down to those at the bottom of the ladder. But if foreign aid is to effect genuine improvement, we must concentrate on the most needy, develop skills for working with them, and allocate resources and funds for that purpose.

The corollary problems—land reform, unemployment, usury—will be enormous. But at the bottom of the ladder we come to terms with the *causes* of underdevelopment. Specialized personnel and equipment will be required, but the encouraging thing about this work is that a relatively small investment produces results that can be seen and measured.

As long as the principal focus of the foreign aid program remains where it is today, fixed largely on loans at the top, the world will continue to ask: *"For whom do you really stand?"*

Through foreign aid, the United States is on trial today

before the world's more than 1 billion neglected people. They want more evidence that we are on their side.

We Must Utilize the Power of Women and the Village Home

Women make up more than half the population of the underdeveloped countries. Since they filter the ideas, bring up the children, pass along the traditions, they are perhaps the most potent force in the emerging nations. Yet in many places, they are not considered in the development process.

No program can succeed unless it includes women. One part of our foreign aid program, namely home economics, is aimed at helping the women of developing nations to better themselves and their families. However, it is surprising, in view of the importance of women's role in today's world, to learn that home economics is only a stepchild of foreign aid. It is the area which proportionately receives the most meager financial support, the first to feel the swinging axe of the budget cut. This surely has been one of the most glaring deficiencies in our setup.

"Foreign aid is a man's world," was the way one administrator summed it up.

"We've been slow to learn that the woman holds the key to most development situations," said Dr. Catherine Holtzclaw, director of AID's home economics department, when I talked to her in September, 1964. "By 1958, we had laboriously built up our overseas staff to a total of 304 home economists. We had to fight to get support and to make a place for each one. At our peak, we had one home economist to every twenty male technicians. We were beginning to see results.

"Then came the budget cuts. They hit us first and they hit us hardest. When it was all over we were left with a remnant of forty-six specialists who must scatter their efforts over eighty countries.

"Let's take Latin America, for example, where the need is especially great, and many doors are open to us. Today, in that vast continent, we have but one home economist. Singlehanded, she is trying to serve Brazil. We've just had to steal one from Colombia, in order to return to Iran one of three specialists that country demands.

"The African countries and the Near East are calling for them. The Congo has four and each of the West African countries has two or three. Iran, one of the neediest and one of the most responsive countries, for a while had none until we remedied that situation slightly as I've just explained.

"In Thailand, we have one woman in ratio to one hundred and thirty men."

To a large degree, farming in the West has become a commercial enterprise, combining labor, machinery, and capital to produce goods for the world market. But in all developing countries, farming is still a way of life, a family occupation. As such, it is a complex of family practices, social customs, taboos, and traditions.

We cannot properly understand the importance of home economics in the foreign aid program unless we have a reasonably accurate picture of the peasant woman's daily life in many underdeveloped countries.

The greater part of her day is spent toiling side by side with her husband in the fields. If she has a baby or two, she carries them slung from her back.

She has been up since before daybreak and very soon thereafter has performed her first chore, grinding the grain or corn for the family's food. In Africa, she rolls her rice, wheat, corn, or millet over a flat stone; in India and other lands, many still grind grain with the stone mill, as used in biblical times.

That done, she will walk a half mile or so to draw water from a well and carry it home in a vessel balanced on her head. She then builds her fire between three stones on the floor, on which she cooks the gruel or bakes her unleavened bread.

If the family is favorably enough situated, the older children are sent off to school, the younger ones dressed to go to the field with the mother. There she works all day, weeding, working the earth with a heavy hoe, cutting the grass or weeds with a sickle, carrying home the vegetables, fruit, or grain when they are ripe.

But her work is not ended. She must build her fire again, perhaps fetch more water, cook the evening meal for her hungry husband and children, and use the remaining daylight hours to clean the house and do what other chores her strength allows her. There is very little time for sewing, mending, or making clothes. When clothes need washing, she takes them to a pond or stream where she has only cold water and rocks as equipment.

Home economics does not mean to this woman what it does to her sister in the West—new fads, more labor-saving devices, in an already scientific kitchen; more aesthetic embellishments and new ways to bring the spice of variety to jaded palates.

It means starting to better her lot with such elemental steps as adding bricks to her stove, or putting longer legs on a bench to relieve her tired back from stooping so often. It means finding ways to get the smoke out of the house, to make her children healthier, to obtain books for them, to cut down on the diseases that kill her chickens, to grow a bigger vegetable patch in her kitchen garden.

Perhaps the situation is put in perspective by this letter to *Rural Missions* from Mrs. Y. Chitombo, wife of a village pastor and volunteer home economist in Southern Rhodesia.

> Whenever I have asked members of the twenty-five women's clubs that I visit, "What is your major reason for working?" I never have failed to get this answer: "So we can have food to eat."
>
> Like the women of many other developing countries, the women of Southern Rhodesia are considered a lesser class. Yet they carry much responsibility for training and supporting the family. The same attitude applies to education: men first. It is only recently that the women have begun striving to make their contributions to a changing country. It is the women largely

who will determine the success or failure of our programs for betterment.

Dean Flemmie Kittrell of the Home Economics Department of Howard University, who has been abroad on several foreign aid assignments, has deep convictions on this point. She stated the following:

> In the United States, home economics is mostly confined to food preparation, sewing, handicrafts, and home decoration. Abroad we should give it an additional dimension, "education for better living."
>
> The family is the primary agency that influences the health and personality of everyone. The family therefore has the biggest job in the world, since it functions at the source from which we build our democratic ways of life.
>
> Home economics then must include not only the physical side—food, health, and handicrafts—but every facet of family life in all its spiritual, biological, aesthetic, and community aspects.
>
> Mankind now has the knowledge to solve most physical problems. The question is, will we put that knowledge to the best possible use? "Man cannot live by bread alone."

Mrs. Jessie Taylor, an AID worker home from Nepal, said to me: "In the long run, the future of a country is shaped more by the women than by the politicians. The impermanence of much of our work and the lack of initiative will change when we devote a better portion of our aid, personnel, and funds toward the development of thrifty and attractive village homes."

In March, 1964, I found a surprise witness for home economics in the person of Harper Johnson, veteran AID specialist just back from Iran. He had been giving me an exciting account of the fight against wheat smut, and I was about to leave his Washington office when he called me back and said:

"There's something I forgot—it's the women. Home economics didn't come to Iran until 1957. That was five years too late. But the whole AID program began to move better from that time on.

"Much more of foreign aid should be focused on the woman's job. When our first workers went out to Iran in 1952, they found the Near East Foundation already there with a small but excellent program in home economics as one of its bright spots.

"Our own program had tough going the first years. But it really received a shot in the arm when our home economics gals moved in and began to win popular support."

He smiled, and continued:

"Women are canny, you know. They can do a lot with little. One of our first home economists left Teheran the third day after she arrived and went out into one of the remote villages. There she found an empty hut. With help from the neighbors, she started to fix it up, adding windows for light, putting in a hard surface floor, and splashing whitewash liberally. When they had it all renovated, they turned it into a women's meeting place where they held cooking and child care demonstrations, classes in vegetable gardening, hygiene, and so on. At the same time, our other home economists were training Iranian women to be home agents.

"After four years, they planned a public exhibition of food products, garments, and handicrafts, all the work of Iranian village women. Knowing how much it would mean if the Shah came, he was sent an invitation. A reply was received stating that he would come, but due to a heavy schedule he could remain for no more than ten minutes.

"The Shah not only appeared, but he became so excited by the possibilities for improvement in Iranian home life that he stayed for over an hour, in the course of which he delivered a speech of encouragement and gratitude for the home economics program.

"In a way, that afternoon was a turning point for foreign aid. The Shah threw his weight behind the program. That stiffened the backbone all along the line. Now home economics is firmly established as a viable part of the program. Iran has 800 extension workers. One-fourth of them are women."

Everywhere the status of women today is changing. Wherever I go in the underdeveloped countries, I see the evidences of the change. In the Middle East, in Pakistan, women are working in banks and offices alongside men; girls are riding bicycles in African countries where it would have been unheard of a few years before. Women are streetcar conductors in Korea; at a school in Liberia where there was a queue of overflow students waiting hopefully for a chance to get in, more than half were girls.

As early as February, 1861, Matthew Vassar, founder of the college that bears his name, said in addressing the first meeting of his board of trustees: "It occurred to me that the mothers of a country mold the character of its citizens, form its institutions, and determine its destiny."

Women have long been given an equal place in education, especially in colleges of agriculture where the art and science of home economics has been on even footing with courses for men. The combination of women's technical knowledge, devotion, and skill has been a decisive factor in the development of rural life in the United States. It is now our privilege to share this advantage with the women of other countries who are so desperately in need of it. The success of our foreign aid effort requires it, depends upon it.

What proportion of AID funds and AID personnel should be fairly allocated to home economics in a dynamic, all out program? We ought to approach this problem with the realization that the utmost we can do will be no more than a token in the face of the need, although a very vital token at that.

Also, in a realm of endeavor as highly personal as home-life education, we should make it clear that we do not intend to impose any of our own customs on the families of other countries, but rather stand ready to help them without bias and without prejudice as they shape their own ends in accord with their deep-rooted traditions and aspirations.

I have talked about the type of program which would be

most desirable not only with AID personnel experienced in this field, but with national leaders in at least a dozen different countries. From these discussions, it appears that a workable home economics program should emphasize at least these four points:

1. Provide more field work in extension education; in other words, personnel available to move among village women, to determine what their problems are, and how they can be solved, using readily available means.

2. Offer courses in leadership; prepare both paid and volunteer workers to be aware of problems, and provide knowledge and skills with which to deal with those problems.

3. Put more emphasis on rural youth work; that is, make more home economics activities available for girls at the 4-H Club level.

4. Help develop more effective curricula and literature wherever possible—from the village school to college and university levels, including rural adult classes.

The objective of such an expanded program would be to make the village home a more attractive, more stable, and thus a happier place to live. This in turn would provide an atmosphere in which programs for progress on all fronts could effectively go forward.

Following many consultations, I would not hesitate to suggest an allocation of 20 per cent of the foreign aid budget to home economics. A measure of the importance I attribute to this work is the ratio of one woman specialist to five men. That would represent a rather drastic change from the present ratio, which is roughly one woman to seventy men.

We Must Support Village Education

No doubt the most hopeful common characteristic of all developing peoples is their hunger for education. Parents deny themselves food to pay for books and to send their children to school. Those who visit the universities of Africa and Asia are struck by the thousands of malnourished students, wearing threadbare clothes, and carrying armloads of books. Everywhere, millions look upon education as a guiding light that can lead them to their promised land.

This universal desire to learn is one of the bright spots on the horizon. But unless mental hunger is realistically appraised and guided into productive channels, where it would be an asset, it may become a liability, like physical hunger.

It is not my intention to imply that our AID program has altogether neglected education. Agricultural colleges have been built; in some countries, elementary school buildings have been erected; curriculum advisers have been sent out on short-term tours. Nor do I mean to suggest that foreign aid should tackle the whole education problem head on. The job is too vast for that.

There is, however, a priority situation in which, with a moderate expenditure of funds and with those funds directly applied to the roots of development, it would be possible to exert positive influences for the future. I refer to basic education in the villages which will place the village teacher and the school in the mainstream of social and economic development.

Of the people living in villages today, 70 per cent are destined to stay there for the rest of their lives, whether they like it or not. Yet the only education they receive is designed to prepare them for urban fields already overcrowded, to train them for jobs which do not exist, and to make them dissatisfied with their lot. They are instilled with a desire to leave the one place where, with proper preparation, they might lead happy and useful lives, namely their villages.

Interest in rural education has prompted me to ask peasant farmers in many countries what they expect in return for the sacrifices they are making to send their children to school. Some of their answers are: "To prepare them for good jobs." "So they won't have to farm." "To get them ready for high school."

Parents in many lands still look upon the teacher as a

dispenser of book learning whose principal function is to rescue their children from the intolerable conditions of the village, where life is hard and pay is poor. The school is an escape route to the cities or towns.

A certain percentage of young people should continue to seek urban employment, but an educational system that only syphons off potentially productive young people into the ranks of the urban unemployed and leaves the age-old economic and social sores of the village still festering is a burden that no developing nation can bear.

On the other hand, in the type of education which prevailed in our own country during pioneer days, there is much that is applicable to the problems of developing nations today. The life of the community was centered around the little red schoolhouse and the church. Every neighborhood had to have its school. The teacher held a position of honor in the community. It was he who nourished the hopes for a better life and, by the knowledge he imparted to the young, pointed the way to its achievement.

There are three main areas in which foreign aid can give genuine support to education on the village level. These are the village school, the training of village-level workers, and adult education.

The schoolhouse is perhaps the one institution which every village the world over has in common. It may be anything from an attractive modern building of brick or stone to a flimsy hut of woven reed and mud wattles, roofed with palm leaves. But it exists, and it is the one public institution with the greatest influence in implanting and developing essential attitudes.

Wherever opportunity is open, foreign aid should offer help in making the village school—the building, equipment, curriculum, and teacher—the inspiration and center for the whole program of village improvement, instead of the ineffectual or, indeed, competing force that it so frequently is.

Unless the village school can be wholeheartedly enlisted in the struggle for betterment, most of the efforts of the social and economic workers are doomed to failure. Life in the villages will hardly be improved until a generation of young men and young women has been so trained that they choose it as their rightful heritage.

The most important factor in bringing about this change is the attitude of the teacher himself. He must see his role both as teacher and as stimulator for change and progress.

To insure that such attitudes prevail will require a massive program of specialized training for teachers. No substantial progress can be made until those teachers who are inculcated with antivillage concepts of education are either retrained or replaced.

This emphasis will require the introduction of new courses and teacher-training schools with consequent changes in the curriculum. We can be of help, when invited, to offer the services of our top rural school men. They would go not as crash advisers on a blitz visit, the method so often employed in the past, but to work as equals with their opposite numbers in the host countries over a period of years. We must realize, in developing schools, it is one thing to attempt to make people over in our own image, quite another to help them perfect their own institutions.

We might ask: "How will the village teacher find time for these added interests?" I have observed that the teacher functions much better in a professional way when he is bound to the whole village as teacher, prophet, and servant for a better tomorrow.

The upgrading of village life will also call for nothing less than an army of volunteer workers on the village level to supplement the current sporadic visits of the paid official. They are frequently voluntary workers who make their living farming or by a handicraft. As one rural education officer in Nigeria put it: "Give us people who can *do.*"

Men and women are needed as village workers who can plant a tree, cull out a sick chicken, graft a tree, rid a house of insects, build a simple stove, check wheat smut. But to prepare such people calls for a large-scale training program. Many countries do not yet have facilities for this. A few, recognizing the need, have set up special schools, but training is both slow and costly.

These village demonstrators could begin preparation through special courses in village schools and high schools, thus making it possible to train large numbers at minimal cost. For example, basic courses in agriculture and home economics could be offered from which not only the demonstrators would benefit but all young people as well, whether they are destined to go to the city or remain in the village.

Finally, at least three-fourths of the adult population in most of the developing countries is illiterate. Here is the largest audience in the world, approximately 780 million people, waiting and needing the rudiments of education to improve their lives. No means of communication can as yet displace the printed word. But for most of them, it is already too late to achieve functional literacy in special classes, successful though they may be.

Progress cannot wait for a new and literate generation to come upon the scene. We must, therefore, face up to the enormous task of finding a way to provide these people with the information essential to the job of improving their condition.

One answer is adult education on an unprecedented scale. The hope, once again, lies in the village school. It is there; it is waiting. Let it be used seven nights a week, all year long, instead of only a few hours each day, for a part of the year, as it now is. Let it be adequately staffed for the challenging situation that lies at hand. This will cost far less than missing the opportunity by default.

We should realize that many of these people, even though they are illiterate, have unique facilities such as keen memory, manipulation, and imitation. Every tool of communication which we have developed in recent years to such a high degree—the visual and aural aids, lectures and discussions—should be recruited in this worthy cause.

The program should extend along the broadest possible spectrum. One essential part might be called inspirational:

an orientation for the villager to a clearer vision of what the revolution of rising expectations can actually mean, of what he has to contribute to it. He should be given a basic introduction to such subjects as credit, cooperatives, and soil conservation.

Another part of adult education should be cultural. The learner should learn something of his nation's history and his part in the world, as well as his country's traditions. It should include a new approach to handicrafts, by veteran craftsmen, so that the manual arts, instead of dying out as they are now doing, could be reinvigorated and expanded.

Perhaps the greatest part of the program should be devoted to demonstrations, to the introduction of techniques whereby the burden of toil could be somewhat eased, the round of daily life made more attractive, and food production increased.

All of these activities would be directed toward a common goal—the well-rounded improvement of village life.

It is not too much to say that the village, rather than the city, is the fulcrum on which the world's future hangs in balance. From the material standpoint, the farmers of the future, whose output will be a major factor in feeding the world, will do their work best if village life is not only sufficiently productive but socially attractive for them.

9

CROSSROAD DECISIONS

"THE ABILITY to wipe out poverty and hunger is the central fact of our time." When Paul G. Hoffman, head of the U.N. Special Fund made that statement before the World Food Congress in the summer of 1963, he gave new reason for hope to that half of the world now struggling to break the bonds of misery and hunger.

For nearly fifteen years, our government and other nations have been engaged in efforts to help make that hope a reality. From 1951 until the present, some 10,000 foreign aid specialists have gone abroad and returned home. An even larger number of people in the participating nations have worked on the program.

From here on, in our approach to rural development, we no longer need to be theoretical. We have a body of experience on which to build. The suggestions which follow were derived from numerous conversations not only with our own field men and their opposite numbers in other countries, but with hundreds of peasant farmers in the fields.

In attempts to make it function more efficiently, our foreign aid setup has already been overhauled four times. It is now operating under its fifth designation. Yet several crucial decisions must be faced if the agency is to again enjoy public confidence and achieve the measure of thoroughness and stability that the future will require of it.

We should decide to:

1. Stick to our original statement of purpose.
2. Separate the military component from economic aid.
3. Shift the center of gravity from Washington to the field.

We Should Stick to Our Original Statement of Purpose

Many are still asking: "Why are we engaged in foreign aid at all? What do we hope to see accomplished? Do recipient countries really understand what we're up to? Do we ourselves really know?"

In the beginning, the purpose of foreign aid, as expounded by General George C. Marshall, could hardly have been stated more clearly: "Our policy is directed not against any country or doctrine, but against hunger, poverty, desperation, and chaos." There was nothing confusing about that.

President Truman continued in the same vein: "All countries, including our own, will benefit from a program to better use the world's human and natural resources. We call for triumphant action against the ancient enemies of hunger, misery, and despair."

It was only from 1952 on, after reports of disappointment and failure abroad had begun to filter back and Congress had commenced asking questions, that conflicting statements of purpose began to appear. That year, Secretary of State Dean Acheson, addressing Roosevelt Day dinner guests in New York, said in the course of his address: "There is hard-headed self-interest in this program."

In an effort to counteract such statements, John H. Reisner * testified before the House Committee on Appropriations: "A strong country like ours needs to set before

* Former Executive Secretary of Agricultural Missions, Inc.

the world at least one clear example of disinterested service. Under present world conditions this is also the best way to promote our own political and economic interests."

Later that summer, I spent fourteen weeks traveling through India. The country was still struggling to gain its balance after three centuries of colonial domination and the thirty-year struggle for independence.

While our Point Four technicians were trying hard to get the program off the ground, the echoes of Dean Acheson's words were reverberating in the press, in government circles, and in college classrooms. Indians were asking, was Point Four only another form of colonialism creeping in through a side door in disguise? This remark by the Secretary of State was exactly what the Communists, then strong in India, needed to discredit our early foreign aid efforts.

In June, 1957, the late John Foster Dulles, then Secretary of State, said during a Congressional hearing: "Whether we make friends I do not care. I do not care in a lot of cases whether they [recipients of U.S. loans] are friends or not. We are doing these things because it will serve the interest of the United States."

I was in the Middle East and Egypt in the autumn of that year. Statesmen and other leaders were asking: "What is a country's self-interest? Aren't the interests of all people mutual? How can you seek your own self-interest without undercutting ours?"

Perhaps no aspect of foreign aid has cost so much in destroyed confidence and actual financial loss abroad as these galling and discordant proclamations concerning our purpose. Not only do they undermine confidence of people in developing countries; they destroy the morale of our field workers. Agronomists, engineers, doctors, and teachers have left valued careers at home, only to hear their earnest efforts downgraded as part of a program of some vague self-interest or as a facet of the cold war.

Hubert Humphrey defended the original purpose of foreign aid before the Senate in 1963: "If you really want support from people back in the home states you had better get back to the humanitarian side. The public is getting fed up with sending arms to people when what they want is some schools and food."

In 1961, Secretary of State Dean Rusk spoke before the Senate Foreign Relations Committee. With diplomatic astuteness he declared:

> We need no other reason to support these measures than the profound fact that they are right. It is right to do these things because peoples are in need of help, and we are able to help them to help themselves; because their children sicken and die while we have science to save them; because they are illiterate while we have the means of education and knowledge; because their agricultural methods and tools win them an annual income of $50 from the soil while we have the technical skill and capital to help them live like human beings.

In June, 1964, U.S. AID announced the formation of the National Committee for International Development. The Committee consists of one hundred distinguished business and professional leaders who give freely of their time in an advisory capacity.

But the official statement about this distinguished group only served to trouble the waters abroad still more. "The over-all objective," stated a key phrase in the press release, "is to tell of the importance of the United States military and economic aid to the nation's prosperity."

That same week, the *Manchester Guardian* took a more forthright view: "The self-interest idea is a reproach to our intelligence. Man-made economic obstacles are still keeping the 'haves' wealthy and the 'have-nots' poor. Unless we can surmount them, history will record an unflattering opinion of our brains, let alone our hearts."

Gunnar Myrdal, the Swedish social scientist, asks: "Why do Americans want to pretend selfish motives when they really act so generously and from humanitarian impulses? Why let the program be confused in a plethora of conflicting statements, each one shaped or designed to fit some individual mood or political occasion?"

Other Western Views

The Norwegian people knew well the suffering caused by war and the cost of repairing the devastation rained upon their country. When Norway began its modest foreign aid program in 1952, its stated purpose at that time, and one which has not been materially altered, was as follows:

> By the formation of a Norwegian Assistance Project, it is hoped that the attention of the Norwegian people will be drawn to the plight of the underdeveloped nations, resulting in a more active attitude toward aiding these countries.

The government of the Netherlands explains its foreign aid program in this way:

> Underlying our aid and assistance programs is a basic philosophy of several components. The public as a whole supports aid and assistance programs because it feels:
>
> 1. An awareness that newly developing countries are in revolution and expect their aspirations to become reality. For this, outside assistance is necessary.
> 2. A moral obligation to help arrange the present and future world environment in as orderly and prosperous a form as possible.
> 3. An economic aim to improve the world's living standard and purchasing power so that benefits may accrue to the well-being of all nations.

We are recognized abroad as a nation of wealth, of rich inherited resources; compassion and sharing have been at the heart of American tradition since colonial days. It is not only a weakness in foreign policy but a radical departure from our heritage to picture ourselves before the world as "priests working for hire; prophets divining for money." The hour is too late for that; the stakes are too high.

Many Americans have expressed this same view. Msgr. L. G. Ligutti, Catholic Church observer to the FAO, spoke for the heart and mind of the American people in 1953, when he testified before Congressional hearings on the foreign aid budget. He said: "We accept foreign aid as part of our obligation to emerging peoples and not on the basis of what we are going to get out of it."

Chester Bowles, twice Ambassador to India, put it this way: "If all Communists on earth disappeared overnight, the need for helping struggling peoples to achieve a democratic society would still be here." *

Foreign aid, as originally conceived and as thoughtful Americans still view it, is an investment in people and their freedom. It is our commitment to a fearless march with them toward a community of nations, free, prosperous, and secure.

Separate the Military Component from Economic Aid

The Point Four program was just getting under way when war broke out in Korea. Up until that time, all funds were being used for economic aid. The objectives were clear. But the war emergency brought a sharp change both in our aims and in our methods.

When the Technical Cooperation Administration was blended into the Mutual Security Agency to expedite the prosecution of the war, economic and technical assistance expenditures began to be influenced mainly by military considerations.

The major part of economic assistance started flowing not only to Korea, but to countries all along the Communist perimeter—Greece, Iran, Turkey, Afghanistan, Pakistan, and India. Military support took three principal forms: grants of equipment, including arms, trucks, and grading machinery; supporting grants to participating countries to help defray the costs of military training and of maintaining an army; developmental assistance in the form of funds and materials for the building of strategic highways, and the stockpiling of materials.

Those who had followed Point Four from the beginning saw a weakening of both aspects of the program, as economic and military aid continued being combined into one effort.

* Chester Bowles, *Ambassador's Report* (New York: Harper and Bros., 1954), p. 343.

In 1953, this shift was nudged a step further, when all aid, both military and economic, was combined in one agency, the Foreign Operations Administration. This move was a severe blow to economic aid. As one government official said: "Point Four was not actually killed; it was cut back from Point Four to point two and one-half!"

From that day on, foreign aid began to lose its cutting edge as a bold new program. Nations which had looked upon Point Four as a partnership began to view it with caution and mistrust. Some countries accepted whatever help they could get, but were careful not to make commitments to our side.

Alarmed by this trend, Walter Van Kirk, Executive Secretary for International Affairs of the National Council of Churches led a delegation to Washington. The delegates stated: "There is genuine anxiety among our people that the United States technical assistance program, for maximum acceptability abroad, and for continuing support at home, should be kept as clear from military involvements as possible."

The proportion of funds for military defense in our total foreign aid budget shot upward year by year. In 1956, military aid accounted for 70 per cent of our foreign aid expenditures. In 1958, out of a total foreign aid budget of $8.4 billion, only 16 per cent went for actual economic aid.

The peak of the trend was reached in that year. Since then, the proportion for military aid has been slowly reduced. In 1965, we spent 34 per cent of the appropriation for military aid and 66 per cent for economic aid.

The matter of carrying on economic aid as a separate effort and returning responsibility for military aid to the defense department has long had its adherents. Americans who support this view are convinced that economic aid, to be effective, should again stand on its own feet and be carried forward to its original objective as a separate effort. Following are some individual viewpoints:

Senator Mike Mansfield said in 1959, when the foreign

aid budget was before Congress for its annual review: "With this catch-all program, we shall never know which is which and what is what so long as both parts are so hopelessly intermingled as is now the case."

The chairman of a department of rural economics in a Midwest college of agriculture has traveled widely and has participated in aid efforts in three countries. Speaking to me as an objective economist, he said: "There is a mixture of objectives in our aid program with a resulting confusion. One objective is to combat or restrict the expansion of Communism by building up military strength. The other is to help improve the well-being of the masses of poor people in the world. The two are not identical. It should be fairly easy to separate the military part and the economic components of aid. This breakdown and understanding are not only needed, but greatly desired by the people of the United States."

Stanley Andrews, the second director of our foreign aid program, has declared: "Probably no international program in history had such widely based support as did our first concept of Point Four. However, beginning in 1953, and lasting up to this day, the program has become more and more a short-term instrument of foreign policy, mainly to resist Communism, *forgetting that the best way to fight Communism is to help people find a suitable alternative.*"

An Indiana farmer insists: "I urge all possible efforts to differentiate between military and nonmilitary aid. The present practice is too wasteful. At heart the American farmer is generous. But he must be assured that his tax money allocated for foreign aid goes into the war against hunger. That's as plain as I can make it."

The head of a national insurance company: "I grant, there is a military job to be done. But let us be clear. The job of economic aid is to provide plows, food, fertilizers, hospitals, schools. We'd better stop trying to mix the two."

In 1963, the National Council of Churches persistently stated: "The churches support efforts to separate military programs from economic development."

President Eisenhower's Subcommittee on International Policy recorded its opinion in these words:

> If development assistance is to make its full contribution to our security by advancing the well-being, political stability, and independence of the underdeveloped world, the program must be acceptable on its own merits. Attaching defense arrangements brings our motives into doubt and impairs the effectiveness of the program.

In the summer of 1964, Senator J. W. Fulbright, discussing the 1965 foreign aid budget, declared: "We should separate the military component from the economic component of our foreign aid program. There has long been merit in the idea that military aid should be removed entirely from foreign assistance legislation."

Why then, in the face of such opinions, do we continue to carry both programs as one package? One argument advanced is that general objectives, such as the preservation of stable governments in developing countries, along with the freedom to build up free institutions—agriculture, home life, and education—are valid concerns of both the military and economic establishments.

Another assumption is that a single agency can be administered with less overhead. The fact is that greater precision in planning and budgeting would result from separation, and would reduce both overhead and waste. The present budgeting and administrative procedure, for example, brings together a host of representatives from the Pentagon and from other agencies for the making of decisions that are often within the grasp of only a few of those present.

Perhaps one reason for perpetuating this awkward marriage between the two programs during peacetime is that we have developed a pattern. Aid is being used as a "gadget" or instrument in the service of short-term foreign policy. A grant or gift of materials, we assume, can function as a magnet to draw a wavering government into line militarily. And, indeed, the offering of such gifts as military hardware can prove attractive to certain individual national leaders.

But too often this practice amounts to trying to make aid into a device to influence history. We fail correctly to measure the intelligence and power of nationalism in developing countries. Resentment and loss of respect for us result, all too often. Our greatest diplomatic and foreign aid setbacks have come where we have applied a patchwork of military aid to nations with an alien culture, supplemented with feeble attempts at economic aid.

Foreign aid at best can only *supplement* diplomacy, never serve as a *substitute* for it. In attempting to make of it an instrument *of* foreign policy, we rob it of the contribution it can make *to* foreign policy.

A soldier-priest in Vietnam, the Reverend Augustine Lac Hoa, who was called to Manila in September, 1964, to receive the Magsaysay Award, given "for extraordinary valor in the defense of freedom," said:

> Many are asking why the West is not winning in Vietnam. May I draw a comparison. Here in the Philippines, Magsaysay won over the hukbalahaps by a program of compassion and dynamic action, to help them better their condition. That won the hearts and minds of the people.
>
> As to Vietnam my answer is simple: the misplacement of the order of importance. There we are placing priority on the winning of a war rather than the people. Win the people first. I can speak plainly because I am a soldier as well as a priest.

Of necessity, military aid and economic aid operate under different sets of ground rules. As a routine matter, military aid accepts heavy expenditures and imperative methods in the routing of highways, confiscation of land, and the stocking of materials.

Economic aid requires patience, deliberate consultation with the people, the orderly development of local resources, the voluntary cooperation of the farmers, whose stiff backbones ultimately will dictate the success or failure of our adventures.

Heavy military expenditures, often a result of emergency conditions, bring about inflation; inflation strikes hardest against the poor, the college students, the low-salaried workers, and the unemployed. The unequal distribution of privilege under a military regime often results in conspicuous luxury and power for a few, more poverty and bitterness for the multitudes.

Normal economic and political development is almost impossible under these circumstances. H. G. Keenleyside, past president of the Society for International Development, said: "Often the chief foreign aid is in the form of military equipment and training. This fact carries a clear threat to democratic institutions, because it is chiefly the military that will have derived benefit from the inflow of funds and the application of modern technology."

Furthermore, the combination of economic aid with military aid introduces elements of secrecy into the very basic aid processes where free and open discussions are required. The spirit of self-help is indeed delicate; it can thrive only where the atmosphere is open and frank.

We have abroad no less than a thousand top grade technicians, engineers, agronomists, and educators, who, before joining AID, worked under the freedom which all scientists insist upon as their natural right. Not a few are chagrined to find that so much of what they had been accustomed to doing openly is "classified."

Raymond W. Miller testified before the House Committee on Foreign Affairs, in 1953: *

> To use technical assistance to gain defense or political objectives is the best way to destroy its usefulness in creating goodwill, international understanding and cooperation in establishing democratic procedures. This self-evident fact needs wider acceptance.

More than a decade of experience has confirmed the wisdom of this testimony.

Foreign aid cannot serve two masters. Both military and economic aid are being stifled by the present confusion. In most of the world's areas of political tension, a forthright program which would mobilize *all the people* to achieve a

* *Congressional Record,* June 3, 1953, p. 859.

life worth defending will, in the long run, greatly reduce the appropriations necessary for military aid.

Shift the Center of Gravity

Anyone who visited Washington fifteen years ago had a hard time finding the foreign aid headquarters. It was then housed across the street from the Department of State in a small frame building known as "Annex No. 9." The first desk had just been put in place, the first secretary employed. The first letter was still to be written, the first telephone call to be put through. So began the Technical Cooperation Administration, one of the forerunners of the present AID.

The first efforts were scrupulously directed toward helping the developing countries at the village level. Stanley Andrews, the second director, told me proudly: "We had four people working abroad to each one in Washington." It was the policy to keep the center of gravity in the areas of operation. A strong but small hub in Washington served principally for backstopping and the shaping of policy.

Today a visitor would experience no difficulty in finding our foreign aid headquarters. It is now a large bureau in the Department of State, with 2,900 employees plus several hundred related workers in other departments of government. There are roughly three people working in the capital for every four abroad.

"How did this shift in the center of gravity come about?" people are asking. "Is it good?"

Although the original TCA lacked a firm central guiding authority, a fact that Dr. Bennett, the first Director, deplored, it was more of a people-to-people program than any we have had since that time. The program operated with a relatively small budget. It was only when military aid and economic aid were combined, as noted above, that the budget was of necessity greatly increased.

The head of a mission abroad often enjoyed status superior to the ambassador because of the funds at his disposal and the number of employees on his staff. Because the mission administered both military and economic aid funds in a country, it almost became a government in itself. There was misunderstanding and resentment in developing nations as some foreign aid missions attempted to use their power to shape the host country's affairs.

In Washington, bureaucracy burgeoned. More and more offices and staff members were added.

Although today AID is small in comparison with other federal agencies such as the Pentagon or the Central Intelligence Agency, people still wonder why there is so much machinery in Washington when the job is overseas, helping peasant farmers in their homes, fields, and orchards.

The 1961 "turn-around" has made some improvements. But the old bureaucratic stiffness persists. If we may judge from responsible field opinion, Washington is handling administrative matters that could be more appropriately handled by competent men in the field.

"Newcomers to the agency who have not been outside America are making decisions for us," said a field man of long experience abroad. Others complain of the long delays in getting action on matters pending.

It will always be a debatable question as to which responsibilities can best be discharged from Washington and which can best be delegated to missions in the field. But whenever procedures are molded to fit the complexities of a bureaucracy rather than to deal promptly with elemental problems, the program suffers.

In Asia, an administrator, one of the few men who has been with foreign aid since its beginning, was distressed that the 1961 "turn-around" has not done more to reduce bureaucratic control. Reviewing his experience for me, he said:

> I agree, it was a mistake to start Point Four in high gear. We were all neophytes. But mistakes then were little mistakes, and something was always flowing out to the people. There was a job to do and it was urgent. Washington was pushing us to do more and spend more. Newcomers arrived to repeat our

> mistakes. Most of us had learned better. All we needed was a chance to correct our mistakes and to put into practice what we had learned.
>
> The waste of money and manpower was clear to us all. We could have corrected much of it in our own way if given a free hand to do so. Instead we were next asked to play down the small projects. It's surprising what you can do with a few bags of trial seed, fertilizers, and pesticides. These we called "projects that speak." But we were instructed that the new emphasis was on the infrastructure which means roads, dams, water power plants, and factories. We saw the importance of this point of view as a part of the whole program. But our blood boiled when one directive in the mid-1950's said Washington frowned on processing projects which cost less than $50,000.
>
> Now the emphasis is on loans and contracts. As administrators, we are tied to our offices, hundreds of miles from the people. Given a free hand, we could have developed the kind of program the people want most and need most. It is our desire to be loyal, but how can we work effectively as instruments of a system that means well but cannot possibly plan for us at a distance of ten thousand miles?

Foreign aid differs sharply from other governmental programs in that its successful prosecution requires a sensitive balance of science, education, business ability, and diplomacy.

Field people urge that aid be given a more direct and precise approach than we are using. I was alerted to this by the chief of agriculture for an aid mission in Latin America. We were talking about different types of projects, health, livestock, schools, etc. Then he showed me his project book for 1964, a well-bound volume of perhaps two hundred mimeographed pages, and explained:

"We'd like to think the projects are worked out in consultation with the people, but in practice it's hardly that way. A local officer may bring in an idea. If we like it and if it looks like something Washington will buy, I ask him to write it up. Then we may talk it over in staff panel. It next goes to the ambassador for an opinion. If he buys it, we put it into the book."

He continued: "Sometimes the ambassador himself puts an idea for a project in the ear of one of the ministers. When these are all in, our committee gives them a final look and we pick out the ones most likely to get support. We make up the book, which goes to Washington for final scrutiny. There it travels from desk to desk, office to office. Specialists are often sent down for more information—more letters, more reports."

"How long does this process take?"

"From three to fifteen months."

"What does this delay from above on project decisions do to the morale of local leaders?"

He smiled: "You can guess that for yourself."

"Don't project requests come directly from villagers?"

"Very few. We'd like to see the book based on more opinions of the people, but it's mostly an American book."

"Isn't there a better way to run the foreign aid business?"

"Yes. Let government give us clear guidelines of policy. Allow us to present a picture of needs and what the people of a country will do; tell us how much we have to work with and trust the execution to us. We would, of course, expect to submit plans for final authentication. But routine decisions should be made here."

"Wouldn't that mean more permanent staff here?" I asked.

"Yes, that's essential. With the present short-term tenure policy, by the time 1964 projects are rejected or approved, half of us will be somewhere else."

Such administration by remote control makes it almost impossible to work out any kind of program tailored to the requirements and the potential resources of a developing country. Too often the result is an appalling clutter of projects that cannot do a country much good nor do they enhance the image of American competence. Whether projects are large or small, the decisions will be more accurate, if they are made as close to the scene of operation as possible, and after consultation with the people to be assisted.

Another field man now serving in his third country explained: "Government should send only those it can entrust with responsibility. Of course we need a backstop in Washington to determine policy and set limits within which we can operate. We need experts to whom we can turn; we especially need a body of opinion to which we can refer controversial matters. But let the field missions develop their programs in consultation with the host country. If we as administrators can't be trusted to do that, we should be called home and others sent out."

Probably general agreement could be reached on the importance of maintaining an adequate base in Washington for backstopping field operations. Then comes the next question: what proportion of the personnel should be assigned for the purpose?

The methods employed by some of the private agencies with regard to the ratio between headquarters and field responsibilities are deserving of study. One of the larger church mission boards has a staff of 860 physicians, surgeons, engineers, clergymen, university and college professors, agriculturists, home economists, and business managers. This enterprise is backstopped by a staff of 84 based in the United States. A smaller church, with 160 people abroad, has a home base contingent of 15. Foundations, too, use comparably small home base staffs.

Even though no absolute parallel can be drawn between the operation of a governmental program and that of a private agency, the comparisons deserve careful consideration.

The desire of headquarters in Washington to keep a watchful eye on aid operations is understandable. But much correspondence, annoyance and delay over detail, endless travel back and forth, can be eliminated or reduced by placing greater responsibility on field personnel. Missions grow impatient and less efficient as details that they should care for themselves are handled—or mishandled—at headquarters with needless mistakes and delay.

By establishing strong, continuing field missions, the center of gravity for the program could again gradually be shifted. As matters stand, many of our finest technicians are chained to desks in Washington, and operate by remote control. Expenses could be reduced; the program could be speeded up and strengthened if many of these highly skilled people were released to serve on the front lines in the countries where the war against want is being waged.

Some government departments can function successfully under a bureaucratic setup. Foreign aid is not one of them. Its program can only be successfully built on the spot, on a basis of equality with the people who, in the end, can assure its success or spell its failure.

10

PERSONNEL FOR FOREIGN AID

PRESIDENT EISENHOWER'S Draper Committee spoke plainly: "In the end success depends on personnel."

Our fourteen years of experience confirm this statement. In this work, we meet some of the most crucial and humanly important issues ever to engage the minds of men.

Through the years, I have met many of America's finest technicians and administrators in some of the world's most difficult places. Undaunted by heat, sickness, or baffling problems of their jobs, they were striving to live up to the highest standards of public service. Why? Because in foreign aid they found a task of singular urgency, the challenge of a cause greater than themselves.

It is therefore shocking to find that even though we have sent more than 10,000 men and women to do a variety of work in 92 countries, and have expended over $110 billion, we still do not have adequate methods for securing, training, and using personnel.

Since it began, AID has had five personnel directors. The

resulting lack of appropriate policy is a hindrance in securing the best staff persons; it causes injustice to those already employed. In Washington, the rapid turnover is a waste of manpower; abroad, it defrauds the poor who have a right to expect more than a mere change of human scenery.

While there is no easy remedy for this, Congress must bear its share of the blame because of its penchant for keeping appropriations to foreign aid on a year-to-year basis, with admonishments from time to time that the program is to be radically cut back or brought to a full stop.

What Men for Gideon?

Arnold J. Toynbee suggests that since personnel is the "chief base to build on," all foreign aid programs in the world might take a leaf from Gideon's experience * in the Old Testament.

The Lord had asked Gideon to form an army to take the walled city of Jericho, a perilous assignment. Gideon at once assembled 32,000 men, but the Lord said: "They are too many." So he was instructed to apply the timeless test: "Whoever is fearful and trembling, let him go home."

Gideon applied the test; 22,000 went back to their homes. The Lord spoke again, "They are still too many." Gideon then took the 10,000 who remained to the water's edge, where he applied the famous drinking test. As the men drank, 300 remained at attention, lapping water from their cupped hands, keeping sharp eyes on their surroundings and on the horizon. The others went down on hands and knees and became fully absorbed in their gulping. The Lord then said to Gideon: "Take you the 300 that lapped water."

Gideon had applied two rigorous tests: one was alertness to environment; the other, the ability to forsake the conveniences of home, even the drinking cup, and employ the discipline required to live and work under unfamiliar conditions.

One of foreign aid's chief needs is such "men for Gideon."

* Judges 7:2–7.

Before any major project is approved, the chief question is not the money but rather who and where are the men for the job? This test must be applied to participant countries as well as to ourselves.

We must give far more attention to establishing standards of professional excellence, methods of recruiting, and minimum requirements for training and preservice orientation. Colleges and universities are rendering valuable service, but for a work of such magnitude and future significance, much more must be done to coordinate, specialize, and upgrade the courses offered. They should not be based on social theory alone, but should include actual field conditions. Instructors should, as far as possible, be men and women who have had *successful field experience.*

For those who intend to spend their lives working on the American scene, we have established rigorous and explicit screening criteria; we have yet to realize that foreign aid is a new profession requiring entirely new insights, judgments, and adaptations. Although technical knowledge is essential, that asset alone will not assure success. Certain *plus qualities* must be woven into the preparation of each staff member, whether he works in Washington or goes abroad.

The high cost of maintaining an aid worker abroad is another reason why we should screen applicants carefully. Senator Gale G. McGee states that it costs over $25,000 a year to maintain one foreign aid appointee overseas.* Financial prudence alone, therefore, dictates that we send only men and women of outstanding ability; that we take pains to place them where they can make their maximum contributions. Field workers and leaders in participant countries are far from convinced that we are doing this.

It could well mean the sending of fewer people to a given project, especially on some contracts. It is time we realized that success cannot always be expected in ratio to the number of people assigned.

* Report to the House Committee on Appropriations, November, 1963, p. 56.

The director for community development in a West African country underlined the importance of this aspect when he said to me:

> Our requirements are enormous for people who can join hands with us and do things. You send too many administrators and advisers. We have not asked for so many advisers on short tours. To fit them in for the period they are here only slows down our own workers. Do send us those who can hang up their coats, help to do a job, and stay around long enough to see what comes of it all. Incidentally, these are the men who make the best advisers. Too many of your VIP's rushing back and forth as consultants only waste their time and ours!

The Two-Year Obsession

There is a regrettable misconception abroad that a foreign aid assignment means a short-term adventure, a colorful interlude in someone's career whose real life work lies at home. Some weigh a tour of duty overseas as to whether it will be a steppingstone to a better job upon their return. Fortunately there are also many who are prepared to look upon foreign aid as a life work.

For these reasons, one of the first questions asked by anyone considering a post in foreign aid is: "How long will I remain overseas?"

There are mixed opinions. The Department of State, which is currently in charge of this phase of the program, follows this policy: A career worker is normally assigned to a given post for two years. After that, he may be up for assignment to another country. If a strong enough case can be made for him, however, he may be returned to the same country for a second two-year term, or even a third, but not longer.

On the basis of tenure, technicians fall into two classes—career and temporary. Career people are on the two-year basis, subject to reassignment; temporary workers are employed on contract, for periods ranging from a few weeks to two years. Rarely is a temporary assignment for a longer period. Of 2,480 specialists in service abroad in February, 1962, 454 were career workers; 2,026 were reported as temporary.

The two-year tour of duty may lend itself to the diplomatic service where procedures are routine and have been long established, but foreign economic aid is a new field that cannot be categorized, at least not yet. How can workers be expected to grapple with century-old problems under two-year contracts that are supported by funds on a year-to-year basis?

We are oversimplifying the most difficult war in which man has ever engaged when we force upon foreign aid the two-year assignments of the Department of State. These two-year sorties can be little more than beachheads from which we withdraw before anything significant has a chance to happen.

There can be a rich satisfaction in making new friends among the nationals of the host country. Our system of roving assignments, however, removes any chance of doing so. And orientation, when given at all, is usually for men only. It is limited largely to lectures on anthropology, to the writing of reports, and to information on routine government-to-government procedures.

Workers often become homesick because they are not in a position to meet with the local people socially, to enjoy the human side of their job, and to feel the challenge that it offers. In this our foreign aid approach is singularly weak.

Churches and voluntary agencies aim to select only those who can put down roots and learn to see life through the eyes of the people with whom they work. One of their primary obligations is to meet people outside the routine of duty. Many succeed in ways that would not be possible on a short-term basis.

I think of two men who kept on growing professionally throughout their careers. One was an agronomist who worked under a church program in Chile for thirty-six years, in agricultural education, fruit growing, and livestock improvement, after which the government awarded him its highest honor for this type of work.

The other worked under a church in South India, for forty-one years, in poultry, extension education, and leadership training. For twenty-two years, he was a member of the Livestock Development Board of Madras State. Upon his retirement, the Chief Minister traveled two hundred miles to preside at a public function where he was awarded the country's Certificate for Meritorious Service. This could happen only because he remained long enough to enter into a serious working relationship with the people of another country.

Recently in Korea I met an AID biologist. He was in his second year of service and due to return home. "Too many of us," he sighed, "haven't had a chance to find out where we are. We're sent off on another assignment before we have a chance to find out what our job is."

In West Africa, an extension representative said: "As we see this work in its many perplexities, we are drawn to favor a policy of longer service—of fewer but better qualified staff people. If a man is to get to the root of things, he ought to have at least eight to ten years in a country. Our touch-and-go tours annoy the host country by taking up their staff members' time. Short tours are frustrating to our own people too, because they are thus deprived of the satisfactions of achievement."

During the spring of 1964, I met a specialist in Latin America who referred to himself as a "dissected career man." He went on to say that he had worked for two years in Korea, a year and a half in Indonesia, a year in Nepal, and four years in Burma. But during the years, his energies had been dissipated over five regions of the world, in five language areas! Realizing how important language is in Latin America, I ventured: "Do you speak Spanish?"

"No," he said with a shrug. "But I do speak marvelous Burmese!"

In the Philippines, I came upon a situation that was brighter. An agronomist for AID had been there nine years, allowing for family trips home in the meantime. He was at the hub of a dynamic program. Things were moving. Teamed with Filipinos, he was busy in planning, advising, working in the barrios, sometimes reproving, but above all, highly respected by hundreds, from barrio farmers to top government officials. He mused: "I'm scared to think what little I would have accomplished if I'd had to leave after two years—even after four."

A man or woman of extraordinary competence may perform acceptably as a short-term consultant on a purely technical job. The U.S. Department of Agriculture is generous in sharing men and women for such assignments. But they cannot provide a satisfactory substitute for career workers who can understand the people and *remain until a unit of work is completed and the results assayed.*

We should seriously question our practice of catapulting so many workers back and forth. It is seriously questioned by the participating countries.

The period of tenure abroad will be influenced by climate, the preferences of different countries, and a staff member's own specialty. Family problems must also be considered. Our best experience points to close screening, orientation, then longer assignments for all, especially in extension education and for those who help to plan and guide programs.

A seven-year minimum field assignment, with a midperiod for home leave, deserves serious consideration. Much of the first year would be kept free for field orientation and language study, leaving two three-year terms as the minimum for field work in a given country.

Personal Qualifications

In discussions of foreign aid, the personal qualifications of workers are often side-stepped. One mission director insisted that such considerations are unimportant. He said: "The main thing is that a man know his stuff." I have found very few leaders of other countries who would agree with this viewpoint.

While people in the host lands are gracious in their attitude toward those who come to work among them, they often expect qualities which few mortals possess.

Unhurried talks with national leaders in various parts of the world have given me some idea as to the personal qualities which they value most. I offer them below, as gleaned from many conversations.

Versatility

A technician need not necessarily be a Jack-of-all-trades. But he should be able to relate his specialty to the whole fabric of life in the country as well as to the specialties of other workers.

Our typically American array of specialists, each with his narrow discipline, isolated even from the disciplines of others in the same field, often proves puzzling to those in other countries. The peasant farmer is a simple son of nature. He must be a man of many skills. He will respond only to people who convince him that they know more about the job in hand than he does. Peasants watch the various specialists on irrigation, fertilizer use, or sanitation with bewilderment and sometimes seek cover in their familiar traditions because our specialties make life too confusing for them. It is extremely important that technical proficiency be undergirded with wide human understanding and common sense.

A personnel secretary for one of the church mission boards was screening men for work in the South Pacific. In dead earnest, he said: "I am expected to produce men who can work with people, mix concrete, heal the sick, grow miracle crops, help deliver babies, write for publication, speak eloquently, and still find time to burn the midnight oil doing research." What is astonishing is that such all-purpose men are sometimes found!

Intelligence and Integrity

National leaders in developing countries who are of pioneering spirit and personal discipline are the ones most likely to take seriously the piloting of new development programs. One of their principal frustrations is having to carry on with foreign aid people with limited vision, or lacking in insight. They appreciate foreign aid associates who learn the language, study the culture and history, and bring to the program their own contributions of precision and professional background based on knowledge, experience, and reflection.

Observance of Moral and Religious Values

Religion and traditions are at the very heart of life in most developing nations. The people appreciate the reverent and religious person, whatever his faith or creed may be.

We tend to categorize life into segments: religion, business, farming, home life, recreation, and so on. Villagers see farming, religion, home life, and community custom as parts of a unified whole, a neatly woven fabric. The foreign aid workers, too, must be able to see life as a whole.

We weaken the case for democracy if we offer religiously motivated peoples, regardless of their faith, no more than the choice between one form of materialism and another. Religious and spiritual values are a valid part of aid. In extending aid, we must not forget the historic spiritual basis for our nation's strength. It is still true that "righteousness exalteth a nation."

Appreciation for What People Have

However important technical knowledge and improved equipment may be, the new order will have to be homemade. It cannot be imported from another continent. It will be forged by a blending of outside resources with simple tools and skills the people already possess.

To respect and to work with what already exists is one of the foundation stones of enduring progress. Whether we work directly with the villagers themselves or through ranking officers as is often the case, the best way to introduce the new is usually by understanding and appreciating the old.

Sensitivity for People

The foreign expert is rightly chosen because of his technical competence. His may be an impersonal assignment such as deep drilling or reforestation. Since he comes from a culture where technology is pre-eminent to a country where nontechnical attitudes are deeply rooted, it is easy for him to become so preoccupied with the technical aspects that he misses contact with the people.

A program *does* win friends—contrary to what we read in the papers—wherever we avoid exclusiveness or any appearance of being arrogant.

Capacity for Hard Work

All developing countries have their share of "second-mile" people. These people must carry their own load in such a way as to inspire other workers with a sense of mission and urgency. They have only gratitude for the foreign worker who, despite enervating climate and other obstacles, puts in long hours working at their side, coming to grips with their tough problems, making them his own.

One of the first steps in solving the personnel dilemma will be for Congress to place AID, like other departments of government, on a continuing budget basis, so that an adequate personnel policy can be forged.

Personnel *can* be found if we view this world struggle against poverty with the sense of urgency that it deserves. Millions are hungry; they have been hungry for periods of five, ten, or thirty years. Now that they know sufficient food and means for a better life can be produced, how long do we expect them to wait?

Gifted personnel is always in short supply, but we do have the people. A university dean said: "I need all of my staff members, but whenever foreign aid is presented to us with wartime urgency, I would voluntarily offer one-tenth of our top people."

We must balance critical world needs against some of our

marginal options. Prime Minister Harold Wilson points out that the industrialized Western countries, representing only one-fourth of the world's population, are utilizing the services of 99 per cent of the world's technicians. Perhaps we could spare more people than we realize.

"Inner Space" to Explore

Who among us has not been thrilled by the recent explorations into outer space? But these adventures, exciting as they are, must not make us less aware of more immediate explorations to be made on this planet. In foreign aid, we may travel thousands of miles to reach a given country. But the real distance to cross is the gulf of culture, race, color, religion, tradition, and economic status that separates a technician from those with whom he works.

We may join with the sociologist and call this "identifying with the people," or "crossing the culture gap." Whatever we call it, this undertaking is one of the most important items on the agenda for every American working abroad.

In Bolivia, I met an American anthropology graduate student working under an AID grant. "I flew here, 4,000 miles in eight hours," he said. "But after six months I'm still learning how to cross the four-foot distance that separates my interpreter and me when we sit down just to talk. If there's outer space to explore, I suppose you'd call this conquering 'inner space.' "

There is no point in minimizing this problem. Whether we term it "identification," "adaptation," or "cultural adjustment," it is an essential key to success in foreign aid. Those who approach it with informed and friendly casualness are more likely to cross it successfully. Those who pretend it is of no consequence or who are unwilling to make the effort, seldom do. The likelihood of being able to span this "inner space" should be one of the chief considerations in choosing candidates for foreign aid.

Another matter that merits attention is the isolation of too many of our AID offices abroad. This was brought home to me when I visited the minister of health in a Central American country.

"Why do you let them quarantine your AID office up on the tenth floor?" she asked. "That makes it official, but it's not accessible to the people. Really," she observed lightly, "you deserve a spot down on the ground floor—with the Ministry of Welfare. It's not really the location so much as the incongruous image it gives you. Thirty thousand hungry, impatient people within twenty-five miles and you quarantined in your plush quarters on the tenth floor!"

A half hour later I pondered as I walked back to the city: "Why should foreign aid, of all our governmental programs, allow itself to be isolated from the masses it was intended to reach, and be tied to the coattails of diplomacy?"

Foreign aid does not have to compete for status. While entitled to diplomatic rank, its range of interest and concern extends from the ambassador's suite to the peasant's field. I have visited AID headquarters which clearly overshadow, to the point of being offensive, the limited development efforts a host country can make. Others are modest, located in rented quarters where AID staff members can rub shoulders comfortably with local officers and civic leaders who, in the end, must do the work. Invariably this is a great advantage.

Another factor in crossing the "inner-space gap" is the manner in which we assign aid personnel to the overseas task.

All developing countries are restricted by the amount of money they can afford to spend for economic improvement. Trained and experienced people are scarce. National workers are usually underpaid and overworked.

It is right to provide well for those who represent us but respect for the feelings of national workers suggests that we be sensitive in such matters as automobiles for transportation or living arrangements. Four staff members sent out as educational advisers to one country were embarrassed to find on arrival that the generous but untutored coordinator back in the U.S. had provided two new sedans to be shared, and a jeep for each of them. Their poorly paid national counterparts whom they were to advise rode the buses or pedaled bicycles.

A number of American industrial firms now advise their American employees abroad to rent living quarters similar to those occupied by their counterparts. Separate colonies are no longer being built. Some of those already in existence are being disbanded. One oil company pays its American employees abroad a "realistic salary," somewhat in line with salaries of their counterparts; the remaining portion is held back for them on their return to the U.S.

The New Breed of Men

In foreign aid, the most successful worker is the one who can work himself out of a job in the shortest period of time.

Host nations want to rely on their own technicians as soon as possible. The good worker then is the one who prepares others to do his job while he himself moves to new tasks either in the same country or elsewhere.

The paucity of able workers in all countries makes this practice imperative. It is estimated that the developing countries need upward of 1 million new technicians to staff their economic development programs alone. Where will the new brains, the new talents come from? The few formal training centers are working to near capacity. But training takes time, and the output can fill no more than a fraction of the world's needs. We must look further, especially for administrative staff.

Traveling in developing countries I encounter, with increasing frequency, what can only be described as a new breed of men. They have energy, foresight, intellect, integrity. They are as yet little known—even in their own countries. But they are men to be reckoned with tomorrow.

Who and where are they? Some are in the professions, some are minor political figures, but because they are young and inclined to speak their minds on such controversial topics as tax enforcement or other forms of social justice, recognition of their talents and advancement is often denied to them. Liberal in their views, they are often considered suspect by those in power.

In Peru, for example, I met such a young man. He was personable and intelligent, serving as a minor assistant in a district agricultural office. He had both a diploma in agriculture and a university degree in economics. I was puzzled as to why he was not being used in a much more important capacity. His sin, it turned out, was that he had been outspoken in his denunciation of usury and had pressed for the redistribution of land to the Indians who flock to him for aid and counsel.

Similarly liberal-minded workers are to be found in the professions, in education, and in business. Students are also in this group. Among them the torch of democracy burns brightly; the new sense of mission is deeply felt. One meets them in almost every country. They will not join those who would bring revolution by force. Rather, they want an opportunity to work for betterment by peaceful means.

When the old outworn power structures collapse, as they inevitably must, perhaps sooner than some might wish, the work of redevelopment will fall heavily upon this new breed. Nothing is more important than establishing a relationship with them now, while there is still time. These men want quickly to learn the skills of development as well as administration. For them, as David E. Lilienthal says: "The job itself can become the schoolmaster."

In too many countries our foreign aid program is becoming stereotyped and frozen within the status quo, where we ought to be bursting out of the mold and using the talents and abilities of these new and socially responsible hands.

Again, we should be doing more to transplant the spirit of democracy, especially among university students in the participating countries. Grants of funds and donations of equipment have their place, to be sure, but they represent only the *fruits* of democratic free enterprise. *They do not in themselves transmit either its heart or its spirit.*

Much has no doubt been accomplished through the exchange of professors between East and West. But most of these workers have been in the physical sciences—agronomy, soils, engineering, and chemistry—and they have been available for only short visits.

Tomorrow's political ideas are being formed not by agents along the sidestreets of cities, or in village squares, but in the university classrooms. If we are in earnest in wanting the world to follow the ways of democracy, one of the really effective steps we could take is to offer some of our outstanding political scientists and philosophers to serve as professors, lecturers, and writers in universities abroad, not for short academic visits but for periods of from five to seven years.

In Southeast Asia, Africa, and Latin America such men, through their lecturing, teaching, and writing, could contribute significantly to shaping the growth of a new generation of political thinkers. These teachers could do much to win the allegiance of the student mind where military build-up is patently failing. The cost would be fractional; friends would accrue to us; democracy would gain support.

11

THE ADMINISTRATION OF FOREIGN AID

PRESIDENTIAL AND private studies of foreign aid are in agreement on one point. All say: "We must firm up administration."

Senator Mike Mansfield, in voting for the severely slashed budget of 1963–64, said he did so only on the assumption that "major changes in the administration will be made."

The course that has been pursued up until now, however, renders this next to impossible. Unlike other departments of government, AID's life has been kept under constant jeopardy. Financial support has been given by Congress on a shaky, year-to-year basis with threats to stop it altogether. The result has been a record of wavering policies and rapid turnover of personnel both among the rank-and-file and in the echelons of administration. The present Administrator, David E. Bell, who joined in 1962, is the tenth in fourteen years of the agency's existence. Imagine Sears Roebuck and Company, A.T.&T., or a Standard Oil company replacing its chief executive officer almost every year!

That the agency has survived at all is proof of the necessity of the job it has to do. Eugene L. Black, former president of the World Bank, said of the able present Administrator: "If I could wish for David E. Bell one thing, I would wish for him a clear-cut contract for five years in order that he might have the opportunity to put into effect some of the improvements he wants to make."

Frank E. Coffin, until recently Deputy Administrator of AID, declared: "Our administrative ills have stemmed largely from giving a short-term outlook to a long-term problem."

Bernard Baruch observed: "We have never really taken time to think through our foreign aid program and its requirements."

Although all of the studies have urged that administration be simplified, this becomes more difficult because of the complexities inherent in the program. In Japan, they tell the story of a sharpster who was arrested for selling "anti-earthquake" pills. When the judge asked him for an explanation, the fellow answered wryly: "Just what would you prescribe?"

Foreign aid has no counterpart in other departments of our government. In a given country, the aid director and his staff must cope with such disparate problems as how to advance farming methods which have remained unchanged since biblical days, or how to negotiate a loan in seven figures with the host government.

Then there are the differences in conditions confronted in the eighty-four nations where AID operates. Although many of these countries have certain characteristics in common, such as lack of roads, a high rate of illiteracy, and dense population, each also has problems peculiar to itself.

Jamaica, for example, became an independent nation only last year, after three hundred years as a British colony. Much of the infrastructure necessary for development is already there—the roads, hospitals, schools, social services, taxes, and good government.

Haiti, on the other hand, only an hour away by plane,

presents an entirely different picture. Although she won her independence in 1804, becoming the second country in the Western Hemisphere to achieve it, her misery and want can hardly be matched anywhere in the world. One hundred and sixty years of political freedom have failed to bring prosperity because the basic conditions for advancement are lacking.

Every country has its own unique laws, or absence of laws, for the regulation of land ownership, usury, cooperative societies, education, and public health. The economy of some nations is based on a single product—rubber in Liberia, cacao in Cameroon, tin in Bolivia. The individual needs of each nation determine the form of authority necessary for administering our foreign aid program, both in Washington and in the participating countries.

Congress does its best to wield an effective hand over the program, but foreign aid is only one of its thousands of responsibilities. And, perhaps more than many others, aid demands unflagging attention throughout the year. Individual senators and congressmen devote a disproportionate amount of time to it, when the budget is being considered.

The State Department has also assumed an overseeing responsibility for certain of AID's functions. But foreign aid is far too vital to be handled as a part-time job by an agency already top heavy with its own routine and emergency situations.

The President himself must devote considerable time and attention to foreign aid, usually throwing the weight of his office behind the budget to keep it from being too badly slashed.

This shapeless form of administration for a program in which so many Americans have a deep personal interest can produce only bewilderment and mistrust. Overseas it is costing us the respect of many who would be our friends.

A new and fresh approach to the problem of administration seems necessary. The proposal I am about to offer has, in essence, been suggested before, but has never been finally acted upon. In view of the lateness of the hour and the critical state of world affairs, I venture to spell it out in greater detail than has ever been done before.

This proposal is that the government set up a quasi-independent, nonpartisan authority containing two essential features: an autonomous board of directors with headquarters in Washington, appointed by the President and approved by Congress. And, overseas, a joint council or commission in each country where we have an aid program.

The board at home of approximately thirty-six directors would include representatives from both houses of Congress, the State Department, as well as experts in each of the fields in which AID operates. The board would appoint the administrator and take responsibility for his actions.

The council in each country overseas might consist of eight persons, four U.S. citizens, and four nationals appointed by the host government. The exact number would vary with the size of a country and volume of foreign aid work carried on.

A Board for International Development

Such a board, as conceived by those favoring it, would consist of men and women of national reputation, representative of the nation's best brains, judgment and experience in government, science, business administration, agriculture, social science, and education; in other words, those fields relevant to the spheres in which foreign aid operates. The board could not only act for the U.S. Government in matters of policy and program; it could provide a much needed center of reference, counsel, and interpretation for AID executives.

These recommendations are based on the belief that foreign aid will be one of the most important expressions of American purpose in the future. Whether the aid program be large or small, some nonpartisan administrative body seems vital to enable effective discharge of its unique and critical responsibilities. It is difficult to see how the improvements called for repeatedly by study commissions—firm administration, efficiency, a more adequate personnel policy—can be brought about without some such authority.

Our heavy investment in foreign aid, the crucial humanitarian and political stakes involved, call for the highest quality of administration to enable the program to move rapidly and with a minimum of error. This would also enable the Chief Executive and the Congress to discharge their responsibilities to the American public far more acceptably than is being done today.

The relationship between the board and the AID administrator would be similar to that between the board of trustees and the president of a university, or the board of directors and the head of a corporation. The present administrator does have the counsel of various committees from time to time. This feature could be continued, indeed strengthened, under such a board.

By whatever means, the Washington AID staff should have a permanent, objective center of reference. Only such a center could produce the personnel policy which is long overdue and the much needed machinery for objective evaluation of our foreign aid effort. Congress as well as AID must be provided with the findings of impartial, continued program review in order to chart the future.

When a controversial issue arises, as for example, what strings ought to be attached to grants or loans in a given country, AID's staff should have the support of an authority capable of studying and interpreting the issues without fear or favor. Congress is not in a position to provide that service. Nor is the Department of State.

One of the unfortunate recent examples of how conclusions are reached under the present setup is the decision on the Bokharo steel mill in India.

In this case, private capital was not available to finance the mill. Knowing this, two private firms owning major Indian factories including steel mills, Tata and Birla Brothers, advised that the new mill be financed and operated as a government enterprise until a private concern was prepared to take over the job. The issue was not that of government control versus private industry.

The United States was asked for a loan. It was clearly stated that American engineers would be employed in the initial stages of development.

An overburdened Congress debated the loan but was unaware of India's particular situation. The request for the loan was rejected. Thus, without adequate or dispassionate study, we attempted to impress the pattern of our own economy upon a country not in a position to act as we would have done in our circumstances. Consequently, we forced India, the greatest of all uncommitted nations, the world's largest democracy, to turn to Russia for help.

This impulsive action resulted in placing the U.S.S.R. as a shining supporter of economic development before the other developing nations. A board, not so subject to public pressure, and with the time and the commitment to study the subtleties of the situation, would have a better chance of handling such problems with discretion.

As we have noted, the proposal of a quasi-independent agency is not without precedent.

Back in 1953, when the Technical Cooperation Administration began foundering in bureaucracy and partisan interests, a committee of nine distinguished laymen and clergymen appeared before the House Committee on Foreign Affairs with a momentous proposal. Following are extracts from the presentation of the spokesmen, John H. Reisner, Raymond W. Miller, and Msgr. L. G. Ligutti.*

> 1. We heartily endorse the appeal made by the Honorable Lawrence H. Smith, member of the House Committee on Foreign Affairs to set up a nonpartisan government foundation or board to administer our world-wide technical assistance program.
>
> 2. Such a board or corporation would greatly facilitate the participation of the United States universities, business organizations, other departments of government, and voluntary agencies in the program.

* At that time, Mr. Reisner was Executive Secretary of Agricultural Missions, Inc.; Mr. Miller was consultant to the Food and Agriculture Organization of the United Nations and Lecturer in the Graduate School of Business Administration, Harvard University; Msgr. Ligutti was Executive Secretary of the National Catholic Rural Life Conference.

3. It would provide a sound financial basis for the program.

4. The corporation would streamline operations, thus providing a degree of efficiency not always associated with government organizations no matter how good they may be.

5. The board would be readily accountable to Congress for a limited and agreed-upon program of operations. *It would have the backing of the American public* [italics added].

The recommendations received favorable comment from both houses of Congress. The House of Representatives went on record as follows:

> It is the sense of the Congress that there be made, under the direction of the President, an analysis and study of the mechanism where technical cooperation may be established on a long-term basis—separated from other programs—including draft proposals for legislation to establish such a program under the administration of an independent agency or government corporation.*

As recently as February 2, 1964, Dr. C. E. Forker, writing in *The New York Times,* expressed this view: †

> Every American will be deeply affected by the decisions resulting from current discussions on foreign aid. Drastic changes in policy have been proposed. My suggestion is that we, as a government, follow the well-tried formula for building good will; that of establishing what might be called the American Foundation, which could be financially supported by our government, but divorced from political attachment.
>
> Too many patently incompatible facets of foreign aid have been mixed together, some of which legitimately should have political, economic, or military strings attached, and others which are hampered, restricted, and ultimately destroyed by such ties.

There is precedent in our own country on the national level in the Tennessee Valley Authority, and many similar precedents, such as the way state universities' boards of trustees report to state legislatures.

* Sec. 309, Amendment to House Mutual Security Act of June 8, 1956.

† Dr. Forker was Director of the China Medical Board, serving under the auspices of the Rockefeller Foundation. He was also Consultant to the U.S. Secretary of War, assigned to the China-Burma theater.

Perhaps the most exact comparison is to be found in Norway where the government set up such a board, the Foundation for Assistance to Underdeveloped Countries, as early as 1952, and has found no reason to change the blueprint since that time. The Foundation consists of a board of seven appointed by the government. This mechanism is said to be highly successful both in overseeing the program and as an arm in implementing government's policies.

We may well envy the success and good will which Norway enjoys in its foreign aid efforts. Funds from individuals, business firms, foundations, and government, are funneled through the foundation. Monies are expended according to government instructions and accounted for to government.

Naturally, not all is perfect in Norway either. Some criticize the development program because it is too meager and moves too slowly. Others feel that Norway has its own poor who should be cared for "before sending succor to those abroad, however great the need may be." Nevertheless, the general feeling is one of valuable and gratifying achievement.

One of the greatest needs of foreign aid for the future is more voluntary service. A quasi-private board could well inspire more top grade people to come into the program as volunteers. The churches in their overseas efforts today are enjoying the advantage of the life-time services of extremely competent doctors, surgeons, agriculturists, and college professors who work happily on a cost-of-living basis because they feel they are doing something worthwhile. In a period of much less urgency, at the close of World War I, there was no shortage of dollar-a-year men who served their country with distinction.

I cannot make the point often enough nor with sufficient strength that the struggle against poverty both at home and abroad has much of the urgency of an all-out war. It can hardly be won by costly, slow-moving, and often erring bureaucracy.

Voluntary service is deeply imbedded in American life as one of our finest traditions. We have an unusual reservoir of talent which could be advantageously tapped. To be specific, among the men and women aged sixty or over and who will retire this year there are 126,000 teachers, 3,000 nutritionists, 18,000 college and university faculty members, 32,000 physicians, and 43,000 nurses.

This isn't to say that foreign aid should not be piloted by a core of younger career men and women. Still, there are hundreds of distinguished scholars, engineers, research workers, and master farmers who would retire early and serve their country as associate technicians for periods of at least four or five years. To use the skills and knowledge of these people could save much expense while adding vitality and prestige to the aid program.

It is widely agreed that private enterprise should be more actively involved in developing the economies of the new nations. There is much that only democratic free enterprise can do that government cannot. Such a semiprivate authority using a large contingent of volunteers could serve as an effective body in stimulating and guiding the efforts of private enterprise in the development of a new country.

One example is the Executive Service Corps which was considered last year. This group was to consist of public-minded businessmen willing to leave their enterprises and go abroad as consultants for short periods of time. Such a project would enjoy much better prospects for success under the umbrella of a nonpolitical but government-related authority.

Finally, a separate board could be of direct assistance to Congress in authenticating the budget and accounting for appropriated funds.

The Congress takes its obligation to the taxpayers seriously, resulting in a tremendous consumption of time. Last year, 282 witnesses appeared before Congressional hearings before the budget was finally passed. Printed records of the hearings covered 5,240 pages; this represented a distillation of more thousands of pages and reports prepared by U.S. AID executives. Many top AID executives must give up at least one-third of their time in preparing materials for Congress and following up in support of the budget. This "annual minuet," as some call it, is a costly procedure. The publicity, mostly on the negative side, hardly helps to enhance foreign aid's public image.

It is my view that a board acting for the President, Congress, and the State Department could handle administrative matters with far less cost and far greater precision than exists at present. It would free the top executives of AID to do the kind of job which the urgency of the world situation demands of them.

The prestige value of such a board for foreign aid is not to be discounted. Its reports to government, instructions from the President and Congress on policy, its major decisions on programing and its reports would carry an authority which could uniquely make constructive and inspiring headlines again. Public confidence would certainly be strengthened as well.

A Joint Council in Each Country— Two Shoulders to the Wheel

Too many of us are prone to think of foreign aid as a one-way street. We advance loans and provide experts on the assumption that our country is on the giving end, the other no more than a recipient.

Albert Mayer, Development Consultant to the Government of India for twelve years, is among those who question this assumption. He says:

> My own experience is of a two-way traffic. We who participate get as good as we give or better: We deliver our own kinds of special experience; we are repaid in unique experience and rewards of another kind, often touching the deeper issues of life.*

At best, it is difficult for individuals of different cultures to understand each other and work freely together; it is even more difficult for two nations. Unless there is complete

* *Pilot Project in India* (Berkeley, Calif.: University of California Press, 1958), p. 122.

communication, misunderstandings arise, even over small matters. One party may feel it is being pushed around or "used."

Aid must be a mutual process: a joint effort with the shoulders of both countries put to the wheel. Frequent overhauls of the AID organization through the years have only made it more and more an impersonal government-to-government program; the people-to-people give and take that was originally intended has diminished, indeed, has almost disappeared.

One way to improve this condition would be to establish a *joint council* in each country, consisting of carefully selected U.S. citizens and nationals as equals. The U.S. ambassador might act as chairman.

If loans, contracts, or grants for technical assistance or any of the various forms of aid are to be genuinely productive, questions such as these must be thoroughly examined from the viewpoints of both parties: (1) What are the resources of the host country in skills and materials? (2) What have we to contribute that could be used profitably? (3) How can we reach those most in need? (4) How can the volume of trade be increased to the *benefit of both countries?* (5) How can our aid program be more effectively related to the work of the U.N. and other agencies?

Only with full discussion by equals who understand the situation can conclusions be reached as to what each side can best contribute, what each can expect to see accomplished, and how soon. Change and development can take place much more rapidly than many of us think, if we place competent men on the job with freedom to plan and act.

We must clarify with firmness and precision the terms on which aid may be given, and the results to be expected. Such a joint council could best do this and could help affirm our conviction that foreign aid is serious business. Its members would have to be of stature equivalent to that of college presidents, administrators in business and education, scientists, executives, and heads of corporations. To spare such people for overseas service would entail some sacrifice. But it would be the best foreign aid investment we could make. The host country would also be invited to draw the most able men from among its own citizens.

The advance to a joint council could be made without serious delay in the AID program or radical change in its structure. The major change would be to transfer certain responsibilities now held in Washington to the joint council. This in turn would free some of our key people now in Washington for more creative work out in the field.

In countries where the host government is weak or unpopular, the joint council could give the AID program much wider support and a more viable base than it has at present.

In theory, our ambassador in a country is the head of AID activities. But when it comes to carrying out the job, he has two strikes against him. The average term in a country for an ambassador is only two years and three months. That hardly gives him enough time in which to deal effectively with AID problems either from the standpoint of perspective or experience. His many compelling duties limit the amount of time he can give the AID endeavor. He must rely heavily on recommendations of the mission in the country, many of whose members, like the ambassador, are itinerant.

A joint council, as suggested here, could better carry out the functions of our AID missions, and provide a backstop for AID workers in the field. It could forge a program and projects for the ambassador that would bear the hallmarks of mature study and judgment. For the benefit of Washington headquarters, the council could supply the quality of field planning and follow-up so critically needed. It would assure seasoned experts who would remain in the host country long enough, as one fieldman put it, "to feel the heat and sweat of what's going on."

Another crucial area is our need to relate our foreign aid effort effectively to the work of others, such as the U.N., foundations, business firms, and voluntary agencies. The present setup does not accomplish this.

In Formosa, the Joint Commission for Rural Reconstruction offers us a solid precedent for such a council. In 1948, Congress created the JCRR, consisting of two Americans and three Chinese. The members were selected with the use of highly rigid standards; they were then accorded the power to act. They reported regularly to the United States Government on their success or failure in carrying out its policies.

In the beginning, everyone thought the situation in Formosa was hopeless. Usury was universal; farmers were enchained by their debts. Even though half of them were tenants and revolt festered, landlords resisted all efforts for land reform. Health services and schools were meager. The island, with a population of 850 per square mile, was overcrowded to begin with. Then, during the late 1940's and early 1950's, more than 2 million refugees poured in from the Chinese mainland.

In spite of these obstacles and others which slowed the rate of development in Formosa, notable progress has been made. Tenancy has been reduced from 50 per cent to 15 per cent; usury has been curbed, and moderate interest rates established. Agricultural betterment has begun. Industries have developed; schools and health services have been expanded and improved.

A member of the Joint Commission said: "The Chinese, better than we, knew what was most needed, and the rate at which they could go ahead. There's nothing so effective as working with people who know and understand."

Formosa is often featured as Exhibit A in current aid reports, but the major share of credit is due to the *choosing of a joint commission of able men from both sides and entrusting them with responsibility for getting the job done.*

In practice, we ask a recipient country to present a plan as a prerequisite for the allocation of funds for a given project. Wherever a country does formulate its own plan, it would only remain for our joint council to tailor and administer our contribution in ways best suited to supplement that plan. But too often the plan is only on paper. The real test comes when steps must be taken to receive and make use of arriving materials and personnel. Too often costly technicians arrive in the field before adequate plans have been made for using them. Fieldmen name faulty planning and lack of follow-up as the commonest shortcomings of aid in action.

The recent shift toward loans and contracts as central components of the aid program is compounding this weakness. In the late 1950's, loans to developing countries made up only 15 per cent of the aid program; today they constitute 60 per cent. It is estimated that by 1966 they will rise to 80 per cent of the total funds. What are the implications of this increase of loans in terms of administration? One loan of $4.5 million, for example, went to a small country and was designated for the purpose of providing credit to peasant farmers. The loan could have had enormous potential if properly followed up. But of the two fieldmen who sponsored it, one was due for transfer and the other was due for home leave and reassignment after a year on the scene. Since the country in question has neither the experience nor the machinery for extending credit to small farmers, the prospect of deriving real benefit from the loan appears dubious.

The United States expects to get back both interest and principal. But the improvement that comes about as a result of the investment is significant. The loaning of a few billion dollars can hardly be considered foreign aid in itself. World banking institutions can also do that. The question for us is: Are the loans achieving worthwhile objectives? Grave doubts have already arisen.

As one indication of how voluntary personnel and private enterprise could help, we have hundreds of successful rural bankers in the U.S. accustomed to tailoring credit programs to meet specific needs. They are familiar with farmers and farming; they know when to be lenient and when to be strict. They have saved many a farmer from disaster and started him on the road to economic health. I do not doubt that a sizable number of these men would respond to a summons by a joint council. A joint council as a permanent administrative fixture in a participating country could make use of such men, especially in the initial stages of a farm loan project.

Foreign aid by contract is not a new direction for aid. But the rate at which contracts are multiplying, and the wide variety of agreements calls for wisdom, planning, and supervision that neither an overworked ambassador nor a transient AID mission can provide.

Here again the distressing fact is not the waste of dollars alone, but the methods of personnel selection and administration so shockingly substandard for a program which has the mandate "to help the least fortunate of the human family to achieve peace, plenty, and freedom."

The contract area of foreign aid, for all its potential, could end in failure, unless more sustained and expert attention is given to clarifying specifications and to supervision at the field level. Until this can be done, we might do well to negotiate fewer contracts, make certain that they are of superior quality, and properly clear them in advance, with the host country.

The importance of wise planning cannot be overemphasized. In the late 1950's, AID proposed an extension program to the Ministry of Agriculture, in Guatemala, for assisting farmers. Consultation led to a plan for employing eighty agents on a five-year basis, to develop an American-type of extension program. The United States and Guatemala were each to contribute $180,000 in 1960. The U.S. share was to decline year-by-year, coming to an end in 1964.

It was hoped that as the agents proved their usefulness to farmers, the Guatemalan Government would voluntarily increase its share, so that by 1965 it would be able to assume all costs. In the intervening years, agents have done their part. Even so, the host government, because of lack of available funds, has been unable to contribute more than a small part of the agreed amount. The program is languishing today. This outcome might have been avoided if all factors had been studied in advance, or if the U.S. extension specialist who conceived the project had not been due for transfer.

Study by a joint council or its equivalent would have raised questions in advance: (1) Is the U.S. extension program the best pattern to follow under the circumstances? (2) Is there something unique in the local situation to be considered first? (3) Should such an effort be started in high gear to cover as many of the farmers as possible? (4) Or should it begin on a limited scale, with more agents added as the host government and the people come to recognize their value and find ways for financing them?

Last year, a fieldman in Peru and I were discussing the importance of sound planning and administration as a joint effort between the U.S. and the host country. During our conversation, he said: "You must see our $2 million elephant." A day later he gave me the following account as he showed me around the place.

One day a few years ago, two American technicians, both strangers to Andean Indian culture, were riding over the dusty roads of Peru's altiplano. They were touched by the misery of the Indians, their patches of rocky land, their little huts. They agreed that AID should do something about it. So they hit upon the idea of building a school where Indians would be trained to work among their own people. "It should be the very best," they agreed. "Nothing is too good for those so badly in need of help."

Somewhere along the line, as plans developed, the idea took shape that the more elaborate and elegant the school, the more it would enhance the prestige of the United States. The technicians wrote a memorandum describing the kind of school they thought AID should provide, and brought it to the attention of a busy ambassador. The idea looked workable to him. Officers in the educational department agreed to the proposal. The notion became fixed that the Indian training school should be constructed in the suburbs of Lima for everybody to see.

No one seems to have taken the time to consult with

either the Indians or other informed people to determine the most advantageous type of training center or the best location for it.

The request was passed along to Washington where it was approved. Plans were developed by architects who could hardly have been more remote from altiplano Indians and their ways of life. Two years and $2 million later, there took shape in the suburbs of Lima a cluster of modern buildings on a neatly clipped campus that would have been the envy of any American college president. It was standing there, almost empty of students, but with heavy maintenance expense, removed from the Indians by both culture and distance.

No one seems to know quite how the new institution, so entirely unsuited to its function, came to be built. A center that the Indians could use for training the workers they need could have been built where the Indians wanted it, at about one-twentieth the expense.

Here again capital loss, though important, is not the chief consideration. Other uses will probably be found for the buildings and campus. The real loss is that the Indians —those most in need of help—have not received it, and our prestige in the country suffered. This sad outcome is not a reflection on any individual, but our present system for setting up and administering field projects without full deliberation and advance planning.

The poet Goethe observed: "Nothing is so frightening as ignorance in action."

Zest for getting things moving is a native American trait in which we can take pride. But however good our intentions, errors must be kept at a minimum. Action must be informed and it must be accompanied by follow-up all the way through to completion, if it is to be worthwhile.

We can expect the need for aid to rise as population mounts and as countries develop to a point where funds can be used profitably. Important decisions must be made!

What kind of program can most profitably use both funds and personnel?

What kind of program is most likely to recapture the confidence and the support of the public?

What approaches will best stimulate self-help and genuine economic development, both for the host country and for ourselves?

In Washington and out in the participating countries we must have an administrative structure capable of grappling with these questions.

12

FOREIGN AID AND THE NATIONAL INTEREST

When Point Four began, it was important to move rapidly and establish a "technical aid presence" on a broad front. Although the mistakes made good copy for the press, much was accomplished, and valuable experience was gained. We bought time.

But, as Secretary of State Dean Rusk said: "Too often in foreign aid we have played by ear, with steps governed less by the priorities of a well-planned program than by the pressures of the moment: the need to preserve an alliance, or procure a military base, or save an economy from collapse." *

We have now come to a time for reflection. Many are asking: "Why foreign aid at all?"

From the heated discussions one hears in Congress and in civic groups, two points of view stand out. One is the broad humanitarian interest in aid. Since this is so deeply

* An address before the Annual Meeting of the Society for International Development, 1962.

rooted in American tradition, it will no doubt continue as a guiding force in any future efforts. The other view speaks of our national interest. The fact is, these two views are interrelated. Attempts to separate them usually end in confusion.

Just what is meant by our national interest? Definitions may vary from the romantic idea of easy "give away" to the stern *quid pro quo* of those who demand that each dollar spent must buy us political alignment and military defense from aided countries.

Probably the best definition of the national interest has already been spelled out for us in the Preamble to the Constitution: "To form a more perfect Union, establish Justice, insure domestic tranquility, provide for the common defense, promote general Welfare, and secure the Blessings of Liberty to ourselves and our Posterity."

Our Constitution, debated point by point, was not drawn up with an eye on its usefulness in the market place alone. It was also the determination of the founding fathers to protect the sovereignty of our people—the "inalienable rights" with which man is "endowed by his Creator."

Our country is unique among the nations of the world: we stand neither in the ranks of those whose establishment is centuries old, nor with those only now grasping for a foothold. Our freedom, won but yesterday, unlocked treasures in skill and human resources, as well as material riches.

Only yesterday we felt secure behind the two great oceans that surrounded us like a moat. Now a network of ocean highways and airway bridges that we ourselves have helped to establish, link us intimately with all nations and peoples of the earth. The historic phrase "the Blessings of Liberty to ourselves and our Posterity" takes on new and sobering significance.

At the close of the 1940's, the world became aware of enormous technical possibilities. While the old evils of oppression, indifference, and greed would have to be combated as before, we began to see that a new world could be created where each child would have bread, books, and shelter, and where each man's liberty would be secure.

History began writing a new scale of values whereby a nation's greatness would be measured not by dollars and cents alone, but by its ability to work and grow with the poor half of the world in the struggle to achieve freedom from want and liberty for all. It now requires only an extension of our historic concept of liberty to include other members of the human race.

Three years ago, I was standing with Ambassador A. S. J. Carnahan as he looked out over the teeming city of Freetown, Sierra Leone. He spoke of the rising hope for a better life on the part of the peoples recently freed from colonial rule. Then, quietly, as if to himself, he said: "The poor nations will not turn back from their quest. The rich must not. 'For unto whomsoever much is given, of him shall be much required [Luke 12:48].' "

When we press our national interest this far, a new light begins to dawn. For we are giving it a dimension that extends beyond passing out surplus foods, technical know-how, or grants of money, however important these may be, in an effort to win political alignment. We are thinking not of our immediate physical security, but of our children, their children, and the future generations. Will their world be one in which liberty has been lost? Or will it be one in which the "Blessings of Liberty" are secure?

In the foregoing chapters, I have tried to offer a few suggestions for improvement that will enable our foreign aid program to serve this larger purpose.

We have two alternatives: One is to drift downgrade with our present makeshift program, until we are forced to employ costly emergency measures to deal with massive famine, economic collapse, and the loss of freedom in a number of countries.

The other is to face the long, steady haul, "waging peace and economic development" for ourselves and the newborn nations. This means the dedication of life and money, but it will save us far greater expenses later on. It can gain for us the confidence and good will of millions, and enable us to earn our share of the new markets for farm products and manufactured goods that are sure to follow a good program.

From an economic standpoint, it is estimated that our present aid program provides jobs for 600,000 people in the United States, including 421,000 in manufacturing, 99,000 in agriculture, and 33,000 in transportation. The more developed a country becomes, the better customer it is for the products of our farms and factories. Japan offers a clear example of this. She is producing one-third more food than ten years ago; yet, with her increased prosperity, her purchases of farm products and other goods from us are increasing steadily. I realize that competition is fierce, but the developing countries can prosper and join with us in better trade relations if we will approach the foreign aid task with the imagination and foresight required.

I became aware of the need for this from an unexpected source while I was traveling in India last year. Sriman Narayan, a member of India's National Planning Commission and I were crossing the Mohanadi River in Orissa, in a small boat. I happened to be admiring the way in which the two boatmen kept adjusting their small, tattered sail so we could cross the river against the wind. Sriman spoke first:

"Our greatest unused asset is the skill of such men as these. We have at least fifty million whose hands are unused. We're beginning to think there should be in addition to heavy industry, a middle technology, based upon scientifically made machines to be powered and operated by hand."

When I made no reply, he continued.

"You have many of your top technicians engaged on space research and exploration. Who knows how many?"

"About 300,000 is the estimate," I answered.

"There! Why shouldn't you and we assign the equivalent of 1 per cent of that number to work on the making of technically efficient hand machines, lathes, looms, metal presses, brick plants, small hardware, so these people could be put to work. If they could start making things and get some buying power, we in turn could begin buying from you several times the amount we are now taking. It could be done, I believe, if you people in America and we put behind it the needed skill and brains."

I thought of Walter Lippmann's classic comment about placing in "really strategic places more young men who have in themselves the seedcorn of a better future."

I left Sriman at the Government House an hour later, but his idea of "middle technology" remained with me. By the employment of more research and imagination in the use of hands, new doors to economic and political liberty might be opened for both East and West.

We still have time in which to demonstrate that democracy, with its flexibility and free play of ideas, can come up with the solutions for age-old problems.

The ideal, of course, will have been achieved when foreign aid as such is no longer needed. This is the fond hope not only of our own lawmakers, but of all responsible leaders in new nations. The Talmud says: "The best charity is to prevent a man from having to accept charity; the best alms are those that enable a man to dispense with alms." It would delay all progress, however, to push this point too hard at present.

It is sufficient to recognize that rapidly growing interdependence makes us social, political, and economic partners with all free nations. In the words of John Donne:

> No man is an island, entire of itself; every man is a piece of the continent, a part of the main . . . any man's death diminishes me, because I am involved in mankind; and therefore never send to know for whom the bell tolls; it tolls for thee.

The various religious faiths have spoken out in behalf of a more effective aid program. For instance, on March 24,

1965, Kenneth L. Maxwell testified before the House Committee on Foreign Affairs. He said, in part:

> For some years now the National Council of Churches and its colleagues in the World Council of Churches have been calling for a "strategy of world economic and social development." . . . Can we hope that our Government and the Administration in concern for "the Great Society" will take more cognizance of its meaning not only for our own nation but also for international relations and the world community?
>
> . . . "Greatness" cannot be an island of selfish or uncaring affluence on a small planet where in the economically underprivileged two-thirds, most are ill-fed, ill-clothed, ill-housed, illiterate or ill.*

To Regain Public Confidence

Although any attempt to be objective involves criticism, it has been my purpose to suggest ways for improving our aid program. One final point to consider is the need to regain public confidence both in the United States and abroad. The American people are hungry, not for success stories, but for actual statements based upon need, successes and failures, a clear picture of our efforts in relation to the contributions of host governments and other agencies.

In wartime, we report losses as well as gains. Surely we should do no less in our foreign aid endeavor. More than propaganda or success records alone is required. Many believe that public support for aid will come in almost direct proportion to the amount of factual, objective information that is given. While program changes along the lines already suggested would do much to increase confidence, the people must be better informed. Only a well-informed public can work constantly to make Arnold J. Toynbee's prophecy come true: "Our age will be remembered chiefly . . . for its having been the first age since the dawn of civilization in which people dared to think it practical to make the

* Kenneth L. Maxwell is director of the International Affairs Commission of the National Council of Churches of Christ in the U.S.A.

benefits of civilization available for the whole human race."

Few thoughtful observers expect this endeavor to be simple or romantic, and a better flow of foreign aid information should help to spell out the urgency of the moral and economic challenge ahead.

More information should be made available to religious and civic groups, and to social science classes in high schools. College students should have access to courses dealing with world hunger, and the work of economic development. Foreign aid is one governmental program in which the general public hungers for a sense of participation. Perhaps one of our large foundations would make a grant available for this purpose.

Our Pledge to the Future

Since Point Four began, the world has climbed the first few steps of a long stairway. From the standpoint of the rich countries, the progress may seem insignificant. But as a teacher in Kenya told me: "For us at the bottom, it looks good."

We have at least seen what the fruits of our fields, our laboratories, and our universities can do when skillfully applied. Crop yields *can* be doubled. Malaria *can* be eradicated, rivers *can* be dammed, thriving youth clubs *can* be established, trade relations *can* be strengthened, people *can* help themselves when given the chance.

What a strange paradox if our foreign aid program comes to a grinding halt at the threshold of what appears to be the most exciting, the most fearful, and yet the most hopeful period in the history of man. At the very moment of challenge, a mood of indifference has settled upon us. Congress casually delayed action on the reduced 1965–66 budget until three months of the fiscal year had passed. There was little or no public protest against this crippling delay. For us, it is a crossroad of decision.

From the humanitarian side, Norman Cousins asked whether "A nation conditioned by affluence might possibly be suffering from *compassion fatigue,* or from *conscience sickness,* the peril of narrowing our field of vision to leave out the unpleasant view of life disfigured by hunger [italics added]." *

From the political and economic side, valuable opportunity is being lost both for the developing countries and for ourselves. To go on floundering at the crossroads, failing to make wise and generous use of our abundance and skills for the betterment of all mankind could mean for the rest of the world freedom lost. And for ourselves, an opportunity for moral, political, and economic leadership that might not come again.

Emmanuel Kant's dictum still holds: "A people is free only when it does what it should."

The better road calls for a more realistic and wiser program, appropriate to our strength, and representative of our finest traditions of free enterprise and liberty. It requires us to apply the same boldness and imagination that we are already applying to military defense and space exploration.

This calls for generosity and statesmanship; it calls for our best talents. But our bread so cast upon the waters of the future will perform its work of mercy and freedom abroad, and return to us in the form of renewed faith in the principles on which our country was founded.

* *Saturday Review,* March 25, 1961.

INDEX